Janet Shannon

THE SUBJECTION OF WOMEN

THE SUBJECTION OF WOMEN

JOHN STUART MILL

Introduction by
Wendell Robert Carr

THE M.I.T. PRESS
Cambridge, Massachusetts, and London, England

Original edition published in London in 1869 by
Longmans, Green, Reader, and Dyer
Introduction copyright © 1970 by
The Massachusetts Institute of Technology

First M.I.T. Press paperback edition, November 1970
Second printing, March 1972
Third printing, June 1974
Fourth printing, February 1976
Fifth printing, September 1977

ISBN o 262 13071 8 (hardcover)
ISBN o 262 63039 9 (paperback)

Library of Congress catalog card number: 73-137474

Printed in the United States of America

INTRODUCTION

JOHN STUART MILL'S *The Subjection of Women* is unquestionably the most eloquent, the most ambitious, and at the same time among the most heartfelt pleas in the English language for the perfect equality of the sexes. Skillfully condensing an entire scheme of social ethics into four short chapters, it is, as Frederic Harrison astutely observed, "one of those very rare examples of a short treatise on a weighty topic, packed with accumulated thought, and fused with ardent conviction." [1] What *The Wealth of Nations* is for classical liberalism and *Das Kapital* for socialism, *The Subjection of Women* is for the century-old agitation for women's rights. It provided the movement with a philosophic rationale of cosmic proportions and, more than a century after its publication, stands unchallenged as the most distinguished intellectual monument the cause has yet produced. The present-day Women's Liberation movement is not soon likely to surpass it.

Born in 1806, just as the vast array of early nineteenth century English reform movements was getting underway, John Stuart Mill spent much of his life crusading for unpopular causes. In 1823, at seventeen years of age, he was hailed into court for scattering tracts through the streets of London which not only advocated birth control but actually described a method of carrying it out. Yet, except for this youthful escapade, Mill for the most part expressed his zeal through his writings, which by his death in 1873 had earned him a place in the front rank of Western thinkers. A child prodigy who began Greek at three, Latin at eight, and by the age of sixteen had completed an education that gave him "an advantage of a quarter of a century" over his contemporaries,[2] Mill grew up at the center of "philosophic" radicalism, a movement led by his father James Mill and the venerable legal reformer Jeremy Bentham and distinguished from all other English reform movements of the early nineteenth century by its "scientific" approach to social issues. Between 1824 and 1828 Mill was a vociferous but highly intellectual propagandist for free trade, parliamentary

[1] Frederic Harrison, "John Stuart Mill," *The Nineteenth Century* 40 (September 1896): 500.
[2] J. S. Mill, *Autobiography* (New York: Columbia University Press, 1924), p. 21.

reform, secret voting, and annual elections. As the range of his writings and activities widened, he also supported—among many other worthwhile causes—the removal of legal restrictions against trade unions, the reform of land tenure, the development of co-operatives, and the repeal of the notorious Contagious Diseases Acts, which empowered justices of the peace in certain towns to order suspected prostitutes to undergo a medical examination for venereal disease. His contributions to logic, political economy, ethics, and metaphysics place him among the foremost philosophers of the world—though Mill, like Marx, always insisted that even his most abstract tomes were integral to his fundamental aim of social reform. And his numerous essays specifically on social questions are among the most intelligent, lucid, and provocative in the English language. Written in 1861 and published in 1869, *The Subjection of Women* appeared at the very moment the status of women was beginning to undergo its greatest revolution in modern history. The work unmistakably identified Mill as the herald of one of the most controversial and influential reform movements of modern times.

I

Despite their reputation for ludicrous fanaticism, the advocates of female equality in the late nineteenth and early twentieth centuries waged their wars with a commendable measure of tactical skill and commanded surprisingly broad-based support. No other part of the movement came close to duplicating the antics of Mrs. Emmeline Pankhurst's suffragettes, who interrupted meetings, provoked clashes with police, hurled stones through windows of government offices and shops, and resorted finally to burning churches, railway stations, and other public buildings. And far from concentrating solely on the right to vote, late nineteenth century crusaders for women's rights, like their present-day counterparts, urged an immense variety of reforms. In addition to their protracted battle for the suffrage, they also fought to open the professions—and especially the medical profession—to women; to reform an education system that, in the words of an indignant headmistress, did not train women even "to be wives—only to get husbands"; [3] and to abolish the pervasive discriminations against women in the laws of marriage, the most notorious of which pro-

[3] Quoted in Winifred Holtby, *Women and a Changing Civilization* (New York: Longmans, Green, 1936), p. 53. For general information about the women's

vided that all property of the wife, even if she herself earned or inherited it, belonged automatically to the husband.

On all of these grievances Mill enunciated concise but far-reaching principles. Regarding the right to vote he affirmed unequivocally that "under whatever conditions, and within whatever limits, men are admitted to the suffrage, there is not a shadow of justification for not admitting women under the same." As for the professions and education, Mill advocated "the opening to [women] of all honourable employments, and of the training and education which qualifies for those employments." Concerning laws of marriage in general, he asserted point-blank that "equality of married persons before the law, is . . . the sole mode in which that particular relation can be made consistent with justice to both sides, and conducive to the happiness of both." And about the laws relating specifically to the property of married women, he stated simply that "whatever would be the husband's or wife's if they were not married, should be under their exclusive control during marriage." The law of divorce was the only major grievance of married women in which Mill failed to suggest positive improvements. And even on that issue the chief reasons for his hesitation were fear of lessening the impact of his other proposals and a desire to give women themselves a chance to be heard on the issue. As he told Professor John Nichol of Glasgow, he decided against discussing the question not only because of "the obvious inexpediency of establishing a connection in people's minds" between equality for women "and any particular opinions on the divorce question," but also because he did not "think that the conditions of the dissolubility of marriage can be properly determined until women have an equal voice in determining them." [4]

In his concrete proposals Mill differed little from a host of other writers spawned by the women's rights movement. Similarly, most of the grounds on which he based his recommendations had been staples of advanced liberal thought for most of the nineteenth century. What distinguished *The Subjection of Women* was its typically "Millian" combination of deep passion and high philos-

rights movement I have drawn on Constance Rover, *Women's Suffrage and Party Politics in Britain, 1866–1914* (London: Routledge & Kegan Paul, 1967). Biographical details about Mill, except where otherwise noted, are drawn from Michael St. John Packe, *The Life of John Stuart Mill* (London: Secker and Warburg, 1954).

[4] J. S. Mill, *The Subjection of Women* (hereafter abbreviated *SW*), pp. 53, 80, 43, 47. *The Letters of John Stuart Mill*, ed. Hugh S. R. Elliot, 2 vols. (London: Longmans, Green, 1910), 2: 212

ophy; its relentless concern with questions about human nature, the formation of character, and the psychology of the sexes; its pervasive uncertainty about whether masculine and feminine character were essentially different; and its insistence on the inseparable connection between women's rights and one of the overriding aims of all Mill's mature thought—the moral reformation of mankind. This distinctive combination of qualities serves at once to define the place of *The Subjection of Women* in the voluminous literature on women's rights, to identify it unmistakably with Mill's more general social philosophy, and to account for its peculiar fate during the century since its publication.

II

Like all his thought, Mill's devotion to women's rights arose from a subtle interplay between his abstract philosophical beliefs and his deepest emotional experiences. The philosophical roots of his commitment lay in the Benthamite radicalism he learned from his father James Mill, who educated John almost singlehandedly and whose power to inspire youth was excelled only by his impatience with inept pupils and recalcitrant disciples. Though a follower and close friend of Jeremy Bentham from 1808, James Mill quickly forged a unique brand of utilitarianism, combining a few of Bentham's leading ideas with his own interpretation of the Scottish Enlightenment philosophy he had imbibed while a student at Edinburgh University. He adopted Bentham's dictum that all institutions should be judged according to their tendency to bring about the "greatest happiness of the greatest number," but contrary to Bentham, he insisted further that the only proper procedure for studying society was to discover laws of human nature and from them to deduce conclusions about the collective behavior of mankind. Applying these assumptions to politics, James Mill asserted as an indisputable truth of human nature that all men entrusted with unrestrained power would be sure to abuse it. This malevolence, he inexorably concluded, could be overcome only by making rulers accountable to their subjects by means of frequent elections, secret voting, and a widely expanded electorate.

Having begun his own literary career, at the ripe age of sixteen, primarily as a propagandist for this program, John Mill immediately realized that "every reason which exists for giving the suffrage to anybody, demands that it should not be withheld from women." True, James Mill had suggested in his *Essay on Govern-*

ment that women might legitimately be barred from the suffrage because their interests were included in that of their husbands and fathers—thereby earning himself the eternal wrath of the women's rights movement. But as John pointed out, James Mill had not intended to suggest that women *ought* to be excluded from the franchise; for he was discussing not whether women *should* be refused the right to vote, but only whether they *could* be denied it without sacrificing the securities for good government. And despite the ambiguity in James Mill's argument, John himself, though on every other issue merely a mouthpiece for his father's views, adamantly refused to equivocate. In his first substantial article he leveled a broadside against the prevailing glorification of female submissiveness, roundly condemning the morality that considered "helplessness" and total dependence upon a husband the apogee of "delicacy" and "femininity." If ever a claim of lifelong allegiance to a cause were justified, it was Mill's assertion in the opening sentence of *The Subjection of Women* that he had held his beliefs about female equality "from the very earliest period when I had formed any opinions at all on social or political matters." [5]

In the wake of the mental crisis that in 1826 shook the foundations of his thought, Mill's attitude toward women achieved a new dimension. The principal catalyst was his friendship with Mrs. Harriet Taylor. Twenty-three years of age when she met Mill in 1830, already married four years and the mother of two sons, Harriet Taylor had been stirred by intellectual and emotional longings too rarefied for her stolid husband John, a generous and successful but (in the words of Carlyle) "innocent dull" Unitarian druggist. On hearing of Harriet's frustrations, her minister, W. J. Fox, a longtime friend of the Mills and contributor of the leading article to the first issue of the *Westminster Review*, proposed a dinner party at which the unfulfilled wife could meet London's most promising young philosopher.

Up to the time he met Harriet, Mill's acquaintance with women had been exceedingly narrow. Besides his mother, a beautiful but mindless drudge for her family whose relations with James Mill were never happy, the only women he had known at all well were the brawny, loquacious Harriet Grote (to describe whom, according to Sydney Smith, the adjective "grotesque" was coined) and the forceful Sarah Austin, both wives of older friends. In the pungent language of Carlyle, Mill "had never looked a female creature, not

[5] *Autobiography*, p. 73; J. S. Mill, "Periodical Literature—Edinburgh Review," *Westminster Review* 1 (April 1824): 526; *SW*, p. 3.

even a cow, in the face." Suddenly he "found himself opposite those great dark eyes, that were flashing unutterable things, while he was discoursing the utterable concernin' all sorts o' high topics." Within three years Mill and Harriet had been swept into one of the classic friendships of the nineteenth century. Deep passion, intense emotional yearnings, immediate intellectual rapport, and an abiding sense of common purpose coalesced to produce an exalted union of spirit with spirit. They traveled together on the continent; Mill spent long weekends with Harriet at her country retreat in Walton on Thames; he dined with her twice a week at John Taylor's home during her brief visits to London; and they "had their thoughts and speculations completely in common"—all, apparently, in a relationship of "strong affection and confidential intimacy only." In 1849, almost twenty years after the beginning of their acquaintance, the premature death of John Taylor made marriage a possibility. Accordingly, in April, 1851, after a respectable interval of two years, Mill at last gained the unspeakable blessing of "adding to the partnership of thought, feeling, and writing which had long existed, a partnership of our entire existence." [6]

Notwithstanding Mill's well-known but vastly exaggerated encomiums to her genius, Harriet's specifically intellectual influence on *The Subjection of Women* was slight. True, Mill confided to a female correspondent that "whatever there is in *The Subjection of Women* which shows any unusual insight into nature or life was learnt from women—from my wife, and subsequently also from her daughter." Yet, though Harriet helped to revise his manuscripts, provided constant inspiration, and engaged in unceasing discussions about his projects, she was in no sense the "originating mind behind his work," either on women or on any other subject. Indeed, in one of his more objective moments, Mill himself explicitly denied having adopted his beliefs about equality of the sexes from Harriet, even speculating that the strength with which he held his convictions was "more than anything else, the originating cause of the interest she felt in me." [7]

What Mill did in part owe to his friendship with Harriet, however, was his romantic notion of women's pervasive importance

[6] Quotations from Mill in *Autobiography*, pp. 161, 168. Information about Mill's friendship with Harriet Taylor, as well as quotations from Carlyle, drawn from F. A. Hayek, *John Stuart Mill and Harriet Taylor* (London: Routledge & Kegan Paul, 1951), *passim*.
[7] *Letters of John Stuart Mill*, 2: 214; Francis E. Mineka, "The Autobiography and the Lady," *University of Toronto Quarterly* 32 (1963): 306; *Autobiography*,

in human life and his intense personal commitment to women's rights. The specific function Mill assigned to women was in one sense as old as the ancient wisdom in the Book of Genesis that man should not be alone. But the importance of the sentiment for Mill arose not from its scriptural authority but from the fact that he met Harriet at the very moment he was undergoing the most profound revolution ever to occur in his thought—a revolution that transformed him from a rigid and somewhat pompous dogmatist to an insatiable eclectic. Enthroning "wholeness" as his primary intellectual value, Mill recoiled from his previous habit of slashing opponents' arguments to bits; dedicated himself to searching out the element of truth in even the most uncongenial philosophic systems; and at one point went so far as to assert that "the great instrument of improvement in men, is to supply them with the other half of the truth, one side of which only they have seen." Not surprisingly, Mill immediately saw in Mrs. Taylor the perfection he himself was seeking. To Mill's eyes she "possessed in combination, the qualities which in all other persons whom I had known I had been only too happy to find singly"—"complete emancipation from every kind of superstition" and earnest indignation against social evils together with "noble and elevated feeling" and "a highly reverential nature." [8]

Mill also accorded to womankind in general a critical role in his quest for wholeness. Citing "reciprocal superiority," rather than mere "equality," as one of the fundamental sources of friendship, Mill assured William Bridges Adams that "we are almost as much the natural complement of one another as man and woman are: we are far stronger together than separately, & whatever both of us agree in, has a very good chance, I think, of being true." And in 1832 he wrote to Harriet that "the great occupation of woman should be to *beautify* life: to cultivate, for her own sake & that of those who surround her, all her faculties of mind, soul, and body; all her powers of enjoyment, & powers of giving enjoyment; & to diffuse beauty, elegance, & grace everywhere." [9]

---

p. 173. For the best—and most recent—discussion of the influence of Harriet Taylor on Mill see John M. Robson, *The Improvement of Mankind* (Toronto: University of Toronto Press, 1968), pp. 53–68, which agrees with the conclusions stated here.

[8] *Collected Works of John Stuart Mill*, ed. F. E. L. Priestley, vols. 12 and 13, *The Earlier Letters of John Stuart Mill*, ed. Francis E. Mineka (Toronto: University of Toronto Press), 12: 42; *Autobiography*, p. 130.

[9] *Earlier Letters*, 12: 123–124; Hayek, p. 67.

Besides convincing him that man and woman, as he said of Bentham and Coleridge, were each other's "completing counterparts," Mill's noble infatuation also confronted him with a staggering range of questions about woman's right to self-fulfillment, her responsibilities in marriage, and her relation to a society that, without ever consulting the victims themselves, subordinated woman to man at every turn. Within two years of their meeting Mill and Harriet were exchanging essays on marriage and divorce, and Harriet was asking point-blank what evil would result from "first placing women on the most entire equality with men, as to all rights and privileges" and "then doing away with all laws whatever relating to marriage." As Mill himself asserted, what Harriet brought home to him above all was "the vast practical bearings of women's disabilities," the "mode in which the consequences of the inferior position of women intertwine themselves with all the evils of existing society and with all the difficulties of human improvement." [10]

With a revered martyr to social conventions and legal absurdities constantly before his eyes, Mill ceased to look on the rights of women merely as an abstract theory. He made it a living principle of action. Like an Evangelical consecrated to bear witness in every sphere of life, Mill lost no opportunity either publicly or privately to express his faith. When in 1865 a group of the electors of Westminster asked him to stand for Parliament, Mill fearlessly warned that he intended to act on his conviction that women were entitled to the suffrage on the same terms as men—the first time in history, Mill surmised, that "such a doctrine had ever been mentioned to English electors." He accepted the questionably helpful support of several indomitable women advocates of female suffrage, who covered a hired carriage with placards and drove through the streets of Westminster peeping out from deep inside to observe the effect on voters. After his election he presented to the House of Commons a petition in favor of female suffrage signed by nearly fifteen hundred women. And among his several courageous stands on principle while a member of Parliament, undoubtedly the most influential was his celebrated speech in favor of amending Disraeli's Reform Bill of 1867 to read "person" instead of "man." In 1850 Mill singled out women's rights as "the most important" of "all practical subjects"; and in 1871 he called the condition of women a "still more fundamental question" than nationalization of land, the

---

[10] Hayek, pp. 77–78; *Autobiography*, p. 173.

relationship between labor and capital, and his own pet project of proportional representation. At his death he left £6000, nearly half his total estate, to women's education.[11]

In his private life Mill displayed an equally intense concern. Before his wedding he wrote out a "formal protest against the law of marriage" for conferring on the husband "legal powers and control over the person, property, and freedom of action of the wife"; and he made a "solemn promise never in any case or under any circumstances" to use such powers. He also "declared it to be his will and intention" that Harriet should retain "the same absolute freedom of action, & freedom of disposal of herself, and of all that does or may at any time belong to her, as if no such marriage had taken place." More than any other of his writings, *The Subjection of Women* had its source in the core of Mill's being. Frederic Harrison caught the emotional essence of the work when he described it, along with the *Autobiography* and *On Liberty*, as "red hot within with affection, pity, and passion." [12]

III

If Mill imbued *The Subjection of Women* with his passionate commitment, he argued his case with characteristically rigorous and even austere logic. Bentham and James Mill had stood at the forefront of the movement to develop a "social science" that swept European thought in the late eighteenth century; and his father spared no effort to make John a consummate practitioner of the craft and to impress on him the surpassing absurdity of all who questioned the enterprise. Throughout his life Mill clung to his father's precepts as an unquestioned article of faith. Thus, when he turned his attention to women's rights, he insisted above all else that "the discussion must be a real discussion, descending to foundations, and not resting satisfied with vague and general assertions." Accordingly, the primary object of *The Subjection of Women*, as Mill pointed out in its very first sentence, was to explain the *grounds* of his belief in women's rights, a task that he fulfilled with admirable success. As the *Edinburgh Review* correctly observed, "of all writers on the claims of women Mr. Mill alone has treated the question on its fundamental principles." [13]

---

[11] *Autobiography*, p. 198; Hayek, p. 166; *Letters of John Stuart Mill*, 2: 311.
[12] Hayek, p. 168; Harrison, p. 489.
[13] *SW*, p. 21; "Mill on the Subjection of Women," *Edinburgh Review* 130 (October 1869): 572.

IV

As Mill practiced it in *The Subjection of Women*, a "philosophic" approach consisted essentially of two inquiries: an investigation of history and an analysis of human nature. In his doctrinaire Benthamite days Mill had relentlessly judged all institutions by the sole criterion of whether they contributed to the greatest happiness of the greatest number. But after his mental crisis one of the chief insights he acquired was the importance of historical perspective. The writings of Coleridge in particular persuaded him that "the long duration of a belief is at least proof positive of an adaptation in it to some portion or other of the human mind." [14] Consequently, the first problem Mill examined in *The Subjection of Women* was whether the long survival and widespread existence of male superiority provided an argument in its favor.

In answering this question Mill devoted much of the first chapter of *The Subjection of Women* to lengthy disquisitions on the social organization of early man, the origin of law, and the steps by which society had developed its present institutions. The presence of such inquiries might be thought to associate Mill with the burgeoning science of anthropology (E. B. Tylor published his *Researches into the Early History of Mankind* in 1865 and his *Primitive Culture* in 1871) and to foreshadow the astounding progress that the late nineteenth century made in studying primitive society generally. Yet *The Subjection of Women* marked not the dawn of a new tradition, but the twilight of an old. Like the history of such renowned Scottish Enlightenment thinkers as John Millar and the David Hume of the *Essays*, Mill's account of the past consisted essentially of plausible but unverified conjectures, massive generalizations based more on assumptions about human nature than on historical research, and courageous but foolhardy attempts to discern the overall direction of social progress.

To Mill, however, the results of his inquiry were beyond dispute. The subordination of women to men, he declared, rested upon theory only, not experience, for no other system had ever been tried. It arose, Mill said, "simply from the fact that from the very earliest twilight of human society, every woman . . . was found in a state of bondage to some man." In his view, the present dependence of women, though milder and more humane than in its original form, was nonetheless merely the "primitive state of slavery lasting

---

[14] J. S. Mill, "Coleridge," in *Essays on Politics and Culture,* ed. Gertrude Himmelfarb (Garden City, N. Y.: Doubleday, 1962), p. 122.

on, through successive mitigations and modifications." To justify the subordination of women on historical grounds, Mill maintained, exemplified "the most pernicious of the false worships of the present day," the idolatry of "established custom" and "general feeling." [15]

Far from justifying male superiority, history, in Mill's view, provided a conclusive argument against it. As ready as August Comte or Karl Marx to postulate grand historical trends, Mill affirmed without hesitation that the cardinal feature of his age was the inexorable expansion of freedom. The "peculiar character of the modern world," he said, was "that human beings are no longer born to their place in life, and chained down by an inexorable bond to the place they are born to, but are free to employ their faculties, and such favourable chances as offer, to achieve the lot which may appear to them most desirable." The social subordination of women thus "stands out an isolated fact in modern social institutions," a "single relic of an old world of thought and practice exploded in everything else," as if a "vast temple of Jupiter Olympus, occupied the site of St. Paul's and received daily worship, while the surrounding Christian churches were only resorted to on fasts and festivals." [16]

V

Yet, though Mill felt obliged to weigh the testimony of history, the crux of his method consisted of analyses of human nature. He adhered steadfastly to the Enlightenment tradition which held with David Hume that "all the sciences have a relation, greater or less, to human nature; and that however wide any of them may seem to run from it, they still return back by one passage or another." [17] For Mill, as for his father, all "scientific" social inquiry, whether about economics, government, individual liberty, or women's rights, must ultimately rest on a rigorous scrutiny of human nature.

Unfortunately, however, Mill's psychology, like his history, was by 1869 hopelessly old-fashioned. Held captive by the methods of his father and, indeed, of the entire British empirical tradition since Locke, Mill derived his psychology primarily from a careful scrutiny of his own mental processes, a procedure that he supple-

[15] *SW*, pp. 6–7, 5–6.
[16] Ibid., pp. 17–18, 21.
[17] David Hume, *A Treatise of Human Nature*, ed. L. A. Selby-Bigge (Oxford: Clarendon Press, 1888), p. xix.

mented by endlessly striving to define terms and by imputing to certain time-honored platitudes about human nature the status of psychological truths. Yet, with characteristic honesty, Mill freely admitted the limitations of his method, and he even resolved during the 1840s to write a book on the subject that lay at the base of all his thought—the formation of character. But having abandoned that project after several years of fruitless effort, he continued to work as best he could in a psychological tradition that, for all its contribution to problems now at the center of academic philosophy in England and America, had made little headway in penetrating the dark recesses of human behavior.

For Mill and the tradition from which he came, the basic fact about human nature was its almost infinite malleability. A person's character, Mill believed, resulted not from the unfolding of innate and ineradicable attributes but from environment and education. Like his father and other notable environmentalists such as Locke and Helvétius, he insisted, as he said in *The Subjection of Women*, on "the extraordinary susceptibility of human nature to external influences, and the extreme variableness" even of those "manifestations which are supposed to be most universal and uniform." [18] Even if he sometimes spoke of "original tendencies" for good or evil in human nature, he nevertheless insisted that environment alone determined which of these propensities triumphed. Social institutions, therefore, were in the grandest sense a school of morality—the breeding ground of evil if badly organized, the nursery of righteousness if properly constituted.

This belief in the power of society to mold human nature underlay almost all of Mill's key arguments in *The Subjection of Women*. His basic argument against subordinating women to men, for example, hinged on an assumption that for more than two hundred years had been a commonplace of English political theory and that James Mill had placed at the center of his thought: the inevitable tendency of human beings, when not restrained by appropriate laws and institutions, to usurp power over their fellows. "It would be tiresome," Mill said, "to repeat the commonplaces about the unfitness of men in general for power, which, after the political discussions of centuries, everyone knows by heart, were it not that hardly anyone thinks of applying these maxims to the case in which above all others they are applicable": the inordinate power that the law allows men to wield over women. Mill, however, made the

[18] *SW*, p. 23.

application with a vengeance that more than compensated for the years of oversight. "The almost unlimited power which present social institutions" give to a husband over his wife, Mill asserted, "evokes the latent germs of selfishness in the remotest corners of his nature—fans its faintest sparks and smouldering embers—offers to him a licence for the indulgence of those points of his original character which in all other relations he would have found it necessary to repress and conceal, and the repression of which would in time have become a second nature."

Worse yet, while existing institutions evoked cruelty in husbands, they provided no redress for wives. Under the present laws of marriage, Mill declared, wives could potentially be forced to endure not merely the traditional forms of slavery, but the "worst description" of bondage known to history. Unlike most other slaves, a wife could be made subject to duty "at all hours and all minutes." She could be denied even Uncle Tom's privilege of having "his own life in his 'cabin'." She had no legal means, as existed in some slave codes, to compel the master to sell her. And worst of all, she could not refuse her master even "the last familiarity" but must submit to "the lowest degradation of a human being, that of being made the instrument of an animal function contrary to her inclinations." [19]

Almost to a man, commentators on *The Subjection of Women* have dismissed this dramatic picture of domestic slavery as exaggerated to the point of absurdity. Yet, in so doing, they have missed both the assumptions and the point of Mill's argument. For as he himself constantly pointed out, Mill was describing "the wife's legal position, not her actual treatment." He recognized that most marriages never descended to the brutish level of tyranny permitted by law; he acknowledged, indeed, that the personal affection and common interests usually fostered by marriage often "tempers the corrupting effects of the power" that the law bestowed on husbands. But Mill also insisted that this fact provided no apology for institutions that positively encouraged despotism. "Laws and institutions," Mill emphasized, "require to be adapted, not to good men, but to bad." Actual practices, therefore, had little bearing on the validity of his argument. In accordance with the dictates of his philosophic method, he was developing a highly abstract argument, based on his theory of psychology, about the possible tendencies of human nature in the

[19] Ibid., pp. 36, 37, 32.

environment created by existing laws—just as James Mill had argued in the *Essay on Government* that the occasional existence of a good despot did not gainsay the general psychological fact that unrestrained rulers were likely to tyrannize over their subjects. Alexander Bain pierced to the heart of at least one part of *The Subjection of Women* when he called it "the most sustained exposition of Mill's lifelong theme—the abuses of power." [20]

VI

In addition to basing his critique of existing institutions on principles of human nature, Mill also recognized that the whole debate over women's rights ultimately turned on a crucial point of psychology: whether "masculine" and "feminine" natures differed from one another in any fundamental way. Discussions of women's rights had long been marked by claims and counterclaims about the nature of woman. Yet as the *Edinburgh Review* pointed out in reviewing *The Subjection of Women*, these debates had been carried on "more in the shape of guesses than of argument." And as a result, confusion reigned. "We have been told," the *Edinburgh Review* noted in despair, "that one sex is better and that it is worse than the other; that it is full of intuitive wisdom and intuitive folly; that it is stronger, that it is weaker, that it is purer, that it is wickeder." "In the face of such assertions," the reviewer wondered in bewilderment, "what is the puzzled spectator to do?" [21]

Among all the proponents—as well as the opponents—of women's rights in late nineteenth-century England, Mill alone confronted the question of woman's nature and abilities head on. Virtually every chapter of *The Subjection of Women* bore witness to the conviction he expressed to Alexander Bain that it was "thoroughly time to bring the question of women's capacities into the front rank of the discussion." [22]

Though working in a psychological tradition that provided little help in resolving the issue, Mill carried out the inquiry according to his highest standards of intellectual rigor. At the outset, he made a valiant effort to distinguish between the influence of "nature" and that of "circumstance." Drawing the full implications of his belief

---

[20] Ibid., pp. 33, 38, 35; Alexander Bain, *John Stuart Mill* (New York: Henry Holt, 1882), p. 130.
[21] "Mill on the Subjection of Women," pp. 572–573.
[22] *Letters of John Stuart Mill*, 2: 209.

in the malleability of human nature, Mill denied that "anyone knows, or can know, the nature of the two sexes, as long as they have only been seen in their present relation to one another." What Englishmen called the nature of women, Mill claimed, "was an eminently artificial thing—the result of forced repression in some directions, unnatural stimulation in others." Making no effort to conceal a major problem that plagued every aspect of his philosophy, Mill candidly admitted that the crucial question of feminine character could not ultimately be resolved until headway had been made on the greatest "of all difficulties which impede the progress of thought, and the formation of well-grounded opinions on life and social arrangements"—the "unspeakable ignorance and inattention of mankind in respect to the influences which form human character." [23]

Yet, though conceding the complexities of the issue, Mill nevertheless deployed a formidable array of arguments against the theory of female inferiority. Attempting first to meet his opponents on their own ground, he began by looking at women "only as they already are, or as they are known to have been," without consideration of what they might become. The large proportion of queens displaying superior talents in government satisfied Mill that women possessed eminent qualifications "for the greater functions of politics" and hence also for the more mundane acts of voting and serving in Parliament. He also emphasized that the practical bent and "rapid and correct insight into present fact" generally displayed by women provided a vital corrective to the excessive abstractness of much philosophy and an indispensable help in "carrying out the results of speculation into practice." Even if women were, as some people claimed, more excitable and more inclined to jump from one subject to another, Mill questioned whether the "absorption of the whole thinking faculty in a single subject" was "the normal and healthful condition of the human faculties, even for speculative uses." And in practical matters the "capacity of passing promptly from one subject of consideration to another, without letting the active spring of the intellect run down between the two," appeared to Mill a "power far more valuable" than a mere talent for rigid and exclusive concentration.[24]

Convinced, moreover, that uncertainty "does not forbid conjecture," Mill went on to broach even the question he had pro-

---

[23] *SW*, pp. 22–23.
[24] Ibid., pp. 53, 56, 57, 59, 64.

nounced insoluble—what "natural character" of women would be revealed if all "artificial causes of difference were withdrawn." And despite the inadequacies of his psychological theory, in defining a way to solve the problem Mill displayed his usual acumen. Given the impossibility of isolating human beings from their surroundings, the only way to discover what part of feminine character might be "natural," Mill said, was to trace "the mental consequences of external influences" and to consider whether the circumstances in which a person has been placed were sufficient to account for "what he is." As the leading historian of the concept of femininity has suggested, Mill deserves credit for being among the first to approach the problem of female character in precisely the way subsequent researchers have usually formulated it.[25]

Mill's conclusions were of course predictable. Taking up what appeared to him "the only marked case . . . of apparent inferiority of women to men," that women had produced no work of "philosophy, science, or art, entitled to the first rank," Mill asserted after a long and careful argument that the domestic and social circumstances in which women lived sufficiently explained almost all "the apparent differences between women and men, including the whole of those which imply any inferiority." As for current sentimentalities about the moral superiority of women, and the somewhat contradictory allegation of their tendency to moral bias, Mill dismissed both as the product of blindness to the fact that women's moral character, like their intellectual proclivities, resulted from the circumstances in which they had been placed.[26]

Except for its fervent advocacy of women's suffrage, few arguments of *The Subjection of Women* provoked more disagreement than Mill's discussion of feminine nature. The *Edinburgh Review* spoke for all but the most avid devotees of women's rights in "altogether rejecting Mill's hypothesis that woman is man in petticoats." Though such reactions could be expected from those enslaved by Victorian morality, one significant criticism arose from an unexpected quarter. It came from a man much of whose thought, like that of Mill, presupposed a basic similarity between types of human beings often considered fundamentally different—from Sigmund Freud, who had translated several of Mill's writings, including *The Subjection of Women*, for an edition of his collected works in German. In his technical psychology Freud constantly

[25] Viola Klein, *The Feminine Character* (London: Kegan Paul, French, Trubner, 1946), p. 113.
[26] *SW*, pp. 68, 76.

emphasized that normal and abnormal—and masculine and feminine—were not fundamentally distinct types of personality, but merely points on a continuum, shading imperceptibly into one another. Yet, many years before he developed the concept of penis envy to account for what he regarded as distinctly feminine traits, Freud adamantly maintained against Mill's arguments in *The Subjection of Women* that "all reforming action in law and education would break down in front of the fact that, long before the age at which a man can earn a position in society, Nature has determined woman's destiny through beauty, charm, and sweetness." Though admitting that "law and custom have much to give to women that has been withheld from them," he nevertheless felt that "the position of women will surely be what it is: in youth an adored darling and in mature years a loved wife." [27]

Yet Freud, like Mill's English critics, construed *The Subjection of Women* too simply. Far from being a dogmatic statement of the identity of masculine and feminine natures, Mill's entire discussion of the question was torn by an implicit tension between his concept of women as complementary to man and his desire to affirm the basic equality of the sexes. He had based his whole assessment of women's present character on the assumption that women provided an essential counterpart to the abstractness, narrowness, and rigidity likely to beset philosophers. "Hardly anything," Mill said in a thinly veiled reference to his own experience, "can be of greater value to a man of theory and speculation who employs himself, not in collecting materials of knowledge by observation, but in working them up by processes of thought into comprehensive truths of science and laws of conduct, than to carry on his speculations in the companionship, and under the criticism, of a really superior woman. There is nothing comparable to it for keeping his thoughts within the limits of real things, and the actual facts of nature." [28]

Yet Mill also asserted outright that the present "domestic and social position" of women furnished a "complete explanation of nearly all the apparent differences between women and men, including the whole of those which imply any inferiority." The obvious implication was that the instituting of Mill's reforms would cause these "apparent differences" to disappear. True, Mill provided himself a loophole by using the word "nearly"; and in a

[27] "Mill on the Subjection of Women," p. 602; Ernest Jones, *The Life and Work of Sigmund Freud*, 3 vols. (New York: Basic Books, 1953–1957), 1: 176. For a full discussion of Freud's view of women see Klein, *Feminine Character*, chapter 5.
[28] *SW*, p. 59.

letter to George Croom Robertson he even admitted that "it is not certain" that the present differences between men and women "are not partly at least natural ones, which would subsist in spite of identity of training." Yet the fact remains that two of Mill's most cherished ideals, wholeness and equality, led him to affirm two apparently incompatible versions of woman's relation to man. At times, he honored woman as man's inspiring complement; at others, he insisted on the basic identity of masculine and feminine natures. Ironically, two of the thinkers most dedicated to rescuing great groups of human beings from social exile fell victim to their emotional attitudes on precisely the point at issue in the entire debate over the psychology of the sexes.[29]

VII

For all its painstaking—if sometimes fallacious—logic, *The Subjection of Women* was more than a philosophic treatise. It was also an impassioned secular sermon. For behind Mill's philosophic method, his critique of unrestrained power, and his theories of human nature lay an encompassing moral vision—a vision as characteristic of Mill as the concept of culture was of Matthew Arnold. On a superficial level Mill's ideal of human existence differed little from that of many other English liberals. It consisted in part of a passionate celebration of freedom in the great English tradition of Milton, Adam Smith, and Herbert Spencer. In questions of women's rights, as in economics, the only adequate principle, Mill proclaimed, was "that things in which the individual is the person directly interested, never go right but as they are left to his own discretion; and that any regulation of them by authority, except to protect the rights of others, is sure to be mischievous." "The anxiety of mankind to interfere in behalf of nature, for fear lest nature should not succeed in effecting its purpose," was, he declared, an "altogether unnecessary solicitude." [30]

Yet Mill did not regard liberty merely as a principle of social organization. Drawing once more on his belief in the power of society to mold human nature, he ultimately justified freedom on the grounds that it alone could accomplish his overriding moral aim: the reformation of human character. Not content merely with a negative argument against male superiority, Mill acknowledged in the final chapter of *The Subjection of Women* that many persons, though convinced of the necessity to reform the laws of marriage and willing to concede the invalidity of all the major arguments against equality, might still want to know what "express advantage would be obtained" by removing women's social and political disabilities. In reply, Mill cited as the primary gain "the advantage of having the most universal and pervading of all human relations regulated by justice instead of injustice." And if justice, he continued, prevailed in the relationship between men and women, "all the selfish propensities, the self-worship, the unjust self-preference, which exist among mankind" would be permanently rooted out. "The child," Mill hoped, "would really, for the first time in man's existence on earth, be trained in the way he should go, and when he was old there would be a chance that he would not depart from it."[31]

To be sure, Mill also noted that to give women the "free use of their faculties" would double "the mass of mental faculties available for the higher service of humanity." But after only a brief discussion Mill abandoned that argument and turned once more to the moral effects of female equality, pointing out as yet another advantage of freedom that it would give to the opinion of women a "more beneficial . . . influence upon the general mass of human belief and sentiment." In Mill's view, widening the scope of women's education and activities would discourage their proclivities to religious proselytism, weaken the influence of mere sentiment on their philanthropy, and, above all, make wives into beings far nobler than mere auxiliaries of "common public opinion," Mrs. Grundys who kept their families mired in "that mediocrity of respectability which is becoming a marked characteristic of modern times." And even when Mill climaxed his argument by stating that after the primary necessities of food and clothing, freedom was the "first and strongest want of human nature," he implicitly assumed that freedom, in addition to bringing a sense of being "twice as much alive, twice as much a human being," would also produce a profoundly "ennobling influence." "Whatever has been said or written," Mill proclaimed, "from the time of Herodotus to the present, of the ennobling influence of free government—the nerve and spring which it gives to all the faculties, the larger and higher objects which it presents to the intellect and feelings, the more unselfish public spirit, and calmer and broader views

---

[31] Ibid., pp. 80, 82.

of duty, that it engenders, and the generally loftier platform on which it elevates the individual as a moral, spiritual, and social being—is every particle as true of women as of men."[32]

VIII

The women's rights movement rapidly bestowed on Mill a devotion commensurate to his own dedication to the cause. Millicent Garrett Fawcett, who participated in the struggle for women's suffrage from its beginnings in the 1860s to its culmination in 1918 and then lived eleven years more to record its history, thought it "an enormous advantage to the whole women's movement, not only in England, but all over the world" to have "for its leader and champion a man in the front rank of political philosophers and thinkers." And on Mill's death Lydia E. Becker, whom Emmeline Pankhurst called the "Susan B. Anthony of the English movement," extolled Mill as the person who "dealt the first effectual blow at the political slavery of women." Though other eminent contemporaries, such as Charles Kingsley, Frederick Denison Maurice, and Sir Charles Dilke also devoted much energy to women's rights, it was John Stuart Mill whom the histories of the movement and the memoirs of its leaders revered as the patron saint of female equality.[33]

In view of the adulation heaped on its author, *The Subjection of Women* itself apparently had less direct influence on the women's rights movement in England than might be suspected. True, dramatic claims for its general influence are legion. According to Frederic Harrison, the "practical effect" of *The Subjection of Women* "on legislation, manners, and opinion has no doubt been greater than anything else which Mill gave to his generation." In 1888 Goldwin Smith, though an arch-foe of women's suffrage, called *The Subjection of Women* "the textbook" of the agitation for "female government." Similarly, A. V. Dicey, who by 1909 had turned from an ardent supporter to a "convinced opponent" of votes for women, nevertheless acknowledged that it was the influence of John Stuart Mill that had made him as a young man

---

[32] Ibid., pp. 82, 84, 89, 91, 95, 96–97.
[33] Millicent Garrett Fawcett, *Women's Suffrage* (London: T. C. and E. C. Jack, 1912), p. 16; statement of Mrs. Becker quoted in Helen Blackburn, *Women's Suffrage* (London: Williams & Norgate, 1902), p. 132.

"favor every attempt to extend not only the liberty but also the political rights of women." And as late as 1914 Havelock Ellis testified that in the nearly half a century since the appearance of *The Subjection of Women* "no book on this subject published in any country—with the single exception of Bebel's *Woman*—has been so widely read or influential." [34]

Though such claims may well be correct, they can be verified only through references to *The Subjection of Women* by persons actually involved in the movement for women's rights. And by this standard, what strikes one is not the abundance but the paucity of documentation. Some people, of course, did single out the work for special praise. Miss Emily Gibson, one of the first students to attend Girton College, Cambridge, was "much thrilled" to learn that the examination in political economy would be set by "my saint and hero, the author of *The Subjection of Women*." And according to his *Autobiography*, Bertrand Russell became a "passionate advocate of equality for women" from the time when "in adolescence I read Mill on the subject." [35] Yet by and large *The Subjection of Women*—when mentioned at all—inevitably takes second place either to other works by Mill or to praise of Mill himself as a man of formidable courage and almost celestial nobility.

Mrs. Fawcett, for example, had no doubt that "the growth of [the women's rights movement] and its adaptation to the practical spirit of the nineteenth century are to a very large extent due to the life-long advocacy and guidance of the late John Stuart Mill." But she explicitly attributed Mill's influence not only to *The Subjection of Women* but also to the *Principles of Political Economy*, *Dissertations and Discussions*, *Liberty*, *Utilitarianism*, and *Representative Government*—in all of which, as she correctly pointed out, he "claimed for women the fullest liberty in the practical affairs of life, and showed the mischief, folly, and misery of withholding from half the human race the opportunity of development which nothing but freedom can give." And though she did indeed credit Mill with impressing upon the movement in England its "character of practical good sense and moderation," the text

[34] Harrison, p. 500; Goldwin Smith, "Conservatism and Female Suffrage," *National Review* 10 (February 1888): 744; A. V. Dicey, *Letters to a Friend on Votes for Women* (London: John Murray, 1909), pp. 1–2; Havelock Ellis, *The Task of Social Hygiene* (Boston: Houghton Mifflin, 1914), p. 71.

[35] Barbara Stephen, *Emily Davies and Girton College*, (London: Constable, 1927), p. 231; Bertrand Russell, *Autobiography, 1872–1914*, 3 vols. (Boston: Little, Brown, 1967–1969), 1: 233.

she cited to illustrate these qualities was not *The Subjection of Women* but Mill's speech on the Reform Bill of 1867. Even Havelock Ellis explained the influence of *The Subjection of Women* not so much by its arguments as by the general authority of Mill's reputation. "The support of this distinguished and authoritative thinker," he said, "gave to the woman's movement a stamp of aristocratic intellectuality very valuable in a land where even the finest minds are apt to be afflicted by the disease of timidity." [36]

To be sure, *The Subjection of Women* has continued to be quoted occasionally even up to our own day. But besides the comparative infrequency of the quotations, the work is almost always cited merely on a specific point and is seldom accorded any special authority. It is not, as it legitimately might be, praised as the overarching philosophic rationale for the equality of women; nor is Mill's name used to give added weight to controversial assertions. *The Subjection of Women*, in short, is generally treated as one work among many, not as a sacred text embodying a unique revelation.

Even the fact that in the early twentieth century the work was reprinted several times attests, curiously enough, not to its influence but to its comparative neglect. In the introduction to a 1909 reprint, the ethical humanist Stanton Coit observed not only that the essay had been "out of print for many years" but also that its structure "is by no means so obvious that the ordinary reader can dispense" with "mechanical means to aid him in analysing the argument and keeping the main lines of the thought clearly before him." Thus, intending to benefit the many working women whom the woman's suffrage movement had begun to draw into its ranks, Coit provided a detailed outline of the argument and numbered the paragraphs for easy crossreference between the text and his précis. And in the introduction to an Oxford World's Classics edition of Mill's writings, which bound *The Subjection of Women* with *Liberty* and *Representative Government*, Mrs. Fawcett herself, though a close friend and devoted admirer of Mill, provided an even more revealing testimony to the fate of the work. Mill's books, she acknowledged, "have become classics." But classics, she continued, "are often more talked about than read, and Mill has not escaped from this fate; for it is obvious from references to his writings which appear from time to time that to not a few of those who refer to him and his opinions, he is but a name, a symbol,

---

[36] Millicent Garrett Fawcett, "The Women's Suffrage Movement," in Theodore Stanton, ed., *The Woman Question in Europe* (New York: G. P. Putnam's Sons, 1884), pp. 2–5; Ellis, p. 71.

and nothing more. People, even highly educated people, talk about Mill and his views without reading his books, and obviously without understanding them or his outlook on life." And significantly, Mrs. Fawcett herself, though "giving no second place to woman's suffrage," nevertheless chose *Representative Government*, not *The Subjection of Women*, as the book "which has most application to the problems of the present day." [37]

The reasons for this relative obscurity are not far to seek. Viewed from the broadest perspective, the fate of *The Subjection of Women* was no doubt merely one example of the general decline in Mill's reputation as a thinker which began in the two decades after his death and from which he is only now beginning to recover. The old-fashioned way in which *The Subjection of Women* approached history and psychology, moreover, clearly precluded its being an important source for such later writers on the history of the family and the psychology of the sexes as Havelock Ellis, who unfailingly made use of the latest available research. Equally important, by the time *The Subjection of Women* was published in 1869, Mill's arguments were already commonplace among those involved in the women's rights movement. To these persons what mattered was not the fact that their arguments had been stated, but that it was the renowned John Stuart Mill who had stated them. Though Goldwin Smith claimed with some justice that the arguments used by other champions of female equality were "mere reproductions" of those of Mill, what he failed to recognize was that no one needed to read Mill to learn them.[38]

As we have seen, moreover, the uniqueness of *The Subjection of Women* lay in the high philosophic level on which it discussed its subject. But by and large the woman's suffrage movement had no need for lofty philosophic principles. For in the very year that *The Subjection of Women* was published, the right of women to participate in public life was conceded *de facto* by allowing female householders to participate in municipal elections, and in 1870 W. E. Forster's Education Act also empowered them to vote at school-board elections and even to sit as members of the boards. From that time on, women's suffrage, like male suffrage after the Reform Bill of 1867, became a question not of principle but of tactics, its

[37] Stanton Coit, Introduction to *The Subjection of Women* (London: Longmans, Green, 1909), p. 3 and *passim*; Millicent Garrett Fawcett, Introduction to *On Liberty, Representative Government*, and *The Subjection of Women* (London: Oxford World's Classics, 1912) pp. vi, xiii.
[38] Goldwin Smith, "Female Suffrage," *Macmillan's Magazine* 30 (June 1874): 148.

primary goals being to influence Parliament and to convert in-
creasingly wider sections of the public. Furthermore, like all
missionaries, the advocates of women's suffrage quickly generated
a litany of standard arguments and standard replies to opponents—
a process immeasurably speeded up by the repetitiveness and
patent fallaciousness of most objections urged against the cause. In
1908 Mrs. Emmeline Pankhurst began a speech by warning that
"what I am going to say to you tonight is not new. It is what we
have been saying at every street corner, at every bye-election during
the last eighteen months." She could just as accurately have said
the last thirty-eight years.[39]

Like almost every other widespread popular agitation for reform
in nineteenth-century England, then, the women's rights movement made little use of sacred philosophic texts. It was, indeed,
virtually unique among English reform movements in generating
so exalted a philosophic statement of its aims as *The Subjection of
Women*. The only other comparable writing which comes readily to
mind is James Mill's *Essay on Government*. And interestingly
enough, that work stands in precisely the same peripheral relation
to the agitation for the Reform Bill of 1832 as *The Subjection of
Women* does to the movement for women's rights.

If the cause of female equality did not squander its energy
explicating sacred texts, it unquestionably indulged in hagiography.
And from first to last John Stuart Mill remained its foremost saint,
revered for displaying in Parliament a heroic courage and for
exemplifying throughout his life a moral nobility unsurpassed in
his generation. Appropriately, in a memorial addressed to a
women's meeting held in 1918 to commemorate Mill, Olive
Schreiner declared him to be "the noblest of those whom the
English speaking race has produced in the last hundred years"
and exhorted the audience to remember that "if we wish to use
our power to its noblest end, we shall have to learn the lesson Mill
taught—that the freedom of all human creatures is essential to the
full development of human life on earth." [40] Though deprived of
personal knowledge of the man, we do have the privilege of reading
the work that incarnates most luminously his compelling passion,
his extraordinary philosophic acumen, his deep fear of uncon-
trolled power, his rigorous inquiries into feminine character, and

[39] Emmeline Pankhurst, *The Importance of the Vote* (London: Woman's Press, 1908), p. 2.
[40] S. C. Cronwright-Schreiner, ed., *The Letters of Olive Schreiner, 1876–1920* (London: T. Fisher Unwin, 1924), p. 402.

his unceasing commitment to freedom as the agent of morality. The present-day advocates of women's liberation unquestionably share Mill's passion. It remains to be seen whether they will be persuaded also of the preeminent importance of the qualities by which he tempered it.

Wendell Robert Carr
Concord, Massachusetts
July 1970

THE SUBJECTION OF WOMEN

CHAPTER I

THE object of this Essay is to explain as clearly as I am able, the grounds of an opinion which I have held from the very earliest period when I had formed any opinions at all on social or political matters, and which, instead of being weakened or modified, has been constantly growing stronger by the progress of reflection and the experience of life. That the principle which regulates the existing social relations between the two sexes—the legal subordination of one sex to the other—is wrong in itself, and now one of the chief hindrances to human improvement; and that it ought to be replaced by a principle of perfect equality, admitting no power or privilege on the one side, nor disability on the other.

The very words necessary to express the task I have undertaken, show how arduous it is. But it would be a mistake to suppose that the difficulty of the case must lie in the insufficiency or obscurity of the grounds of reason on which my conviction rests. The difficulty is that which exists in all cases in which there is a mass of feeling to be contended against. So long as an opinion is strongly rooted in the feelings, it gains rather than loses in stability by having a preponderating weight of argument against it. For if it were accepted as a result of argument, the refutation of the argument might shake the solidity of the conviction; but when it rests solely on feeling, the worse it fares in argumentative contest, the more persuaded its adherents are that their feeling must have some deeper ground, which the arguments do not reach; and while the feeling remains, it is always throwing up fresh intrenchments of argument to repair any breach made in the old. And there are so many causes tending to make the feelings connected with this subject the most intense and most deeply-rooted of all those which gather round and protect old institutions and customs, that we need not wonder to find them as yet less undermined and loosened than any of the rest by the progress of the great modern spiritual and social transition; nor suppose that the barbarisms to which men cling longest must be less barbarisms than those which they earlier shake off.

3

In every respect the burthen is hard on those who attack an almost universal opinion. They must be very fortunate as well as unusually capable if they obtain a hearing at all. They have more difficulty in obtaining a trial, than any other litigants have in getting a verdict. If they do extort a hearing, they are subjected to a set of logical requirements totally different from those exacted from other people. In all other cases, the burthen of proof is supposed to lie with the affirmative. If a person is charged with a murder, it rests with those who accuse him to give proof of his guilt, not with himself to prove his innocence. If there is a difference of opinion about the reality of an alleged historical event, in which the feelings of men in general are not much interested, as the Siege of Troy for example, those who maintain that the event took place are expected to produce their proofs, before those who take the other side can be required to say anything; and at no time are these required to do more than show that the evidence produced by the others is of no value. Again, in practical matters, the burthen of proof is supposed to be with those who are against liberty; who contend for any restriction or prohibition; either any limitation of the general freedom of human action, or any disqualification or disparity of privilege affecting one person or kind of persons, as compared with others. The *à priori* presumption is in favour of freedom and impartiality. It is held that there should be no restraint not required by the general good, and that the law should be no respecter of persons, but should treat all alike, save where dissimilarity of treatment is required by positive reasons, either of justice or of policy. But of none of these rules of evidence will the benefit be allowed to those who maintain the opinion I profess. It is useless for me to say that those who maintain the doctrine that men have a right to command and women are under an obligation to obey, or that men are fit for government and women unfit, are on the affirmative side of the question, and that they are bound to show positive evidence for the assertions, or submit to their rejection. It is equally unavailing for me to say that those who deny to women any freedom or privilege rightly allowed to men, having the double presumption against them that they are opposing freedom and recommending partiality, must be held to the strictest proof of their case, and unless their success be such as to exclude all doubt, the judgment ought to go against them. These would be thought good pleas in any common case; but they will not be thought so in this instance.

Before I could hope to make any impression, I should be expected not only to answer all that has ever been said by those who take the other side of the question, but to imagine all that could be said by them—to find them in reasons, as well as answer all I find: and besides refuting all arguments for the affirmative, I shall be called upon for invincible positive arguments to prove a negative. And even if I could do all this, and leave the opposite party with a host of unanswered arguments against them, and not a single unrefuted one on their side, I should be thought to have done little; for a cause supported on the one hand by universal usage, and on the other by so great a preponderance of popular sentiment, is supposed to have a presumption in its favour, superior to any conviction which an appeal to reason has power to produce in any intellects but those of a high class.

I do not mention these difficulties to complain of them; first, because it would be useless; they are inseparable from having to contend through people's understandings against the hostility of their feelings and practical tendencies: and truly the understandings of the majority of mankind would need to be much better cultivated than has ever yet been the case, before they can be asked to place such reliance in their own power of estimating arguments, as to give up practical principles in which they have been born and bred and which are the basis of much of the existing order of the world, at the first argumentative attack which they are not capable of logically resisting. I do not therefore quarrel with them for having too little faith in argument, but for having too much faith in custom and the general feeling. It is one of the characteristic prejudices of the reaction of the nineteenth century against the eighteenth, to accord to the unreasoning elements in human nature the infallibility which the eighteenth century is supposed to have ascribed to the reasoning elements. For the apotheosis of Reason we have substituted that of Instinct; and we call everything instinct which we find in ourselves and for which we cannot trace any rational foundation. This idolatry, infinitely more degrading than the other, and the most pernicious of the false worships of the present day, of all of which it is now the main support, will probably hold its ground until it gives way before a sound psychology laying bare the real root of much that is bowed down to as the intention of Nature and the ordinance of God. As regards the present question, I am willing to accept the unfavourable conditions which the prejudice assigns to me. I consent that established custom, and the general feeling, should be deemed conclusive against me, unless that custom and feeling from age to age can be shown to have owed their existence to other causes than their soundness, and to have derived their power from the worse rather than the better parts of human nature. I am willing that judgment should go against me, unless I can show that my judge has been tampered with. The concession is not so great as it might appear; for to prove this, is by far the easiest portion of my task.

The generality of a practice is in some cases a strong presumption that it is, or at all events once was, conducive to laudable ends. This is the case, when the practice was first adopted, or afterwards kept up, as a means to such ends, and was grounded on experience of the mode in which they could be most effectually attained. If the authority of men over women, when first established, had been the result of a conscientious comparison between different modes of constituting the government of society; if, after trying various other modes of social organisation—the government of women over men, equality between the two, and such mixed and divided modes of government as might be invented—it had been decided, on the testimony of experience, that the mode in which women are wholly under the rule of men, having no share at all in public concerns, and each in private being under the legal obligation of obedience to the man with whom she has associated her destiny, was the arrangement most conducive to the happiness and well-being of both; its general adoption might then be fairly thought to be some evidence that, at the time when it was adopted, it was the best: though even then the considerations which recommended it may, like so many other primeval social facts of the greatest importance, have subsequently, in the course of ages, ceased to exist. But the state of the case is in every respect the reverse of this. In the first place, the opinion in favour of the present system, which entirely subordinates the weaker sex to the stronger, rests upon theory only; for there never has been trial made of any other: so that experience, in the sense in which it is vulgarly opposed to theory, cannot be pretended to have pronounced any verdict. And in the second place, the adoption of this system of inequality never was the result of deliberation, or forethought, or any social ideas, or any notion whatever of what conduced to the benefit of humanity or the good order of society. It arose simply from the fact that from the very earliest twilight of human society, every womàn (owing to the value attached to her by men, combined with her inferiority in muscular strength) was found in a state of bondage to some man. Laws and systems of polity always begin by recognising the relations they find already existing between individuals. They convert what was a mere physical fact into a legal right, give it the sanction of society, and principally aim at the substitution of public and organised means of asserting and protecting these rights, instead of the irregular and lawless conflict of physical strength. Those who had already been compelled to obedience became in this manner legally bound to it. Slavery, from being a mere affair of force between the master and the slave, became regularised and a matter of compact among the masters, who, binding themselves to one another for common protection, guaranteed by their collective strength the private possessions of each, including his slaves. In early times, the great majority of the male sex were slaves, as well as the whole of the female. And many ages elapsed, some of them ages of high cultivation, before any thinker was bold enough to question the rightfulness, and the absolute social necessity, either of the one slavery or of the other. By degrees such thinkers did arise; and (the general progress of society assisting) the slavery of the male sex has, in all the countries of Christian Europe at least (though, in one of them, only within the last few years) been at length abolished, and that of the female sex has been gradually changed into a milder form of dependence. But this dependence, as it exists at present, is not an original institution, taking a fresh start from considerations of justice and social expediency—it is the primitive state of slavery lasting on, through successive mitigations and modifications occasioned by the same causes which have softened the general manners, and brought all human relations more under the control of justice and the influence of humanity. It has not lost the taint of its brutal origin. No presumption in its favour, therefore, can be drawn from the fact of its existence. The only such presumption which it could be supposed to have, must be grounded on its having lasted till now, when so many other things which came down from the same odious source have been done away with. And this, indeed, is what makes it strange to ordinary ears, to hear it asserted that the inequality of rights between men and women has no other source than the law of the strongest.

That this statement should have the effect of a paradox, is in some respects creditable to the progress of civilisation, and the improvement of the moral sentiments of mankind. We now live—that is to say, one or two of the most advanced nations of the world now live—in a state in which the law of the strongest seems to be entirely abandoned as the regulating principle of the world's affairs: nobody professes it, and, as regards most of the relations between human beings, nobody is permitted to practise it. When anyone succeeds in doing so, it is under cover of some pretext which gives him the semblance of having some general social interest on his side. This being the ostensible state of things, people flatter themselves that the rule of mere force is ended; that the law of the strongest cannot be the reason of existence of anything which has remained in full operation down to the present time. However any of our present institutions may have begun, it can only, they think, have been preserved to this period of advanced civilisation by a well-grounded feeling of its adaptation to human nature, and conduciveness to the general good. They do not understand the great vitality and durability of institutions which place right on the side of might; how intensely they are clung to; how the good as well as the bad propensities and sentiments of those who have power in their hands, become identified with retaining it; how slowly these bad institutions give way, one at a time, the weakest first, beginning with those which are least interwoven with the daily habits of life; and how very rarely those who have obtained legal power because they first had physical, have ever lost their hold of it until the physical power had passed over to the other side. Such shifting of the physical force not having taken place in the case of women; this fact, combined with all the peculiar and characteristic features of the particular case, made it certain from the first that this branch of the system of right founded on might, though softened in its most atrocious features at an earlier period than several of the others, would be the very last to disappear. It was inevitable that this one case of a social relation grounded on force, would survive through generations of institutions grounded on equal justice, an almost solitary exception to the general character of their laws and customs; but which, so long as it does not proclaim its own origin, and as discussion has not brought out its true character, is not felt to jar with modern civilisation, any more than domestic slavery among the Greeks jarred with their notion of themselves as a free people.

The truth is, that people of the present and the last two or three generations have lost all practical sense of the primitive condition of humanity; and only the few who have studied history accurately, or have much frequented the parts of the world occupied by the living representatives of ages long past, are able to form any mental picture of what society then was. People are not aware how entirely, in former ages, the law of superior strength was the rule of life; how publicly and openly it was avowed, I do not say cynically or shamelessly—for these words imply a feeling that there was something in it to be ashamed of, and no such notion could find a place in the faculties of any person in those ages, except a philosopher or a saint. History gives a cruel experience of human nature, in showing how exactly the regard due to the life, possessions, and entire earthly happiness of any class of persons, was measured by what they had the power of enforcing; how all who made any resistance to authorities that had arms in their hands, however dreadful might be the provocation, had not only the law of force but all other laws, and all the notions of social obligation against them; and in the eyes of those whom they resisted, were not only guilty of crime, but of the worst of all crimes, deserving the most cruel chastisement which human beings could inflict. The first small vestige of a feeling of obligation in a superior to acknowledge any right in inferiors, began when he had been induced, for convenience, to make some promise to them. Though these promises, even when sanctioned by the most solemn oaths, were for many ages revoked or violated on the most trifling provocation or temptation, it is probable that this, except by persons of still worse than the average morality, was seldom done without some twinges of conscience. The ancient republics, being mostly grounded from the first upon some kind of mutual compact, or at any rate formed by an union of persons not very unequal in strength, afforded, in consequence, the first instance of a portion of human relations fenced round, and placed under the dominion of another law than that of force. And though the original law of force remained in full operation between them and their slaves, and also (except so far as limited by express compact) between a commonwealth and its subjects, or other independent commonwealths; the banishment of that primitive law even from so narrow a field, commenced the regeneration of human nature, by giving birth to sentiments of which experience soon demonstrated the immense value even for material interests, and which thenceforward only required to be enlarged, not created. Though slaves were no part of the commonwealth, it was in the free states that slaves were first felt to have rights as human beings. The Stoics were, I believe, the first (except so far as the Jewish law constitutes an exception) who taught as a part of morality that men were bound by moral obligations to their slaves. No one, after Christianity became ascendant, could ever again have been a stranger to this belief, in theory; nor, after the rise of the Catholic Church, was it ever without persons to stand up for it. Yet to enforce it was the most arduous task which Christianity ever had to perform. For more than a thousand years the Church kept up the contest, with hardly any perceptible success. It was not for want of power over men's minds. Its power was prodigious. It could make kings and nobles resign their most valued possessions to enrich the Church. It could make thousands in the prime of life and the height of worldly advantages, shut themselves up in convents to work out their salvation by poverty, fasting, and prayer. It could send hundreds of thousands across land and sea, Europe and Asia, to give their lives for the deliverance of the Holy Sepulchre. It could make kings relinquish wives who were the object of their passionate attachment, because the Church declared that they were within the seventh (by our calculation the fourteenth) degree of relationship. All this it did; but it could not make men fight less with one another, nor tyrannise less cruelly over the serfs, and when they were able, over burgesses. It could not make them renounce either of the applications of force; force militant, or force triumphant. This they could never be induced to do until they were themselves in their turn compelled by superior force. Only by the growing power of kings was an end put to fighting except between kings, or competitors for kingship; only by the growth of a wealthy and warlike bourgeoisie in the fortified towns, and of a plebeian infantry which proved more powerful in the field than the undisciplined chivalry, was the insolent tyranny of the nobles over the bourgeoisie and peasantry brought within some bounds. It was persisted in not only until, but long after, the oppressed had obtained a power enabling them often to take conspicuous vengeance; and on the Continent much of it continued to the time of the French Revolution, though in England the earlier and better organisation of the democratic classes put an end to it sooner, by establishing equal laws and free national institutions.

If people are mostly so little aware how completely, during the greater part of the duration of our species, the law of force was the avowed rule of general conduct, any other being only a special and exceptional consequence of peculiar ties—and from how very recent a date it is that the affairs of society in general have been even pretended to be regulated according to any moral law; as little do people remember or consider, how institutions and customs which never had any ground but the law of force, last on into ages and states of general opinion which never would have permitted their first establishment. Less than forty years ago, Englishmen might still by law hold human beings in bondage as saleable property: within the present century they might kidnap them and carry them off, and work them literally to death. This absolutely extreme case of the law of force, condemned by those who can tolerate almost every other form of arbitrary power, and which, of all others presents features the most revolting to the feelings of all who look at it from an impartial position, was the law of civilised and Christian England within the memory of persons now living: and in one half of Anglo-Saxon America three or four years ago, not only did slavery exist, but the slave-trade, and the breeding of slaves expressly for it, was a general practice between slave-states. Yet not only was there a greater strength of senti-ment against it, but, in England at least, a less amount either of feeling or of interest in favour of it, than of any other of the customary abuses of force: for its motive was the love of gain, unmixed and undisguised; and those who profited by it were a very small numerical fraction of the country, while the natural feeling of all who were not personally interested in it, was un-mitigated abhorrence. So extreme an instance makes it almost superfluous to refer to any other: but consider the long duration of absolute monarchy. In England at present it is the almost universal conviction that military despotism is a case of the law of force, having no other origin or justification. Yet in all the great nations of Europe except England it either still exists, or has only just ceased to exist, and has even now a strong party favourable to it in all ranks of the people, especially among persons of station and consequence. Such is the power of an established system, even when far from universal; when not only in almost every period of history there have been great and well-known examples of the contrary system, but these have almost invariably been afforded by the most illustrious and most prosperous communities. In this case, too, the pos-sessor of the undue power, the person directly interested in it, is only one person, while those who are subject to it and suffer from it are literally all the rest. The yoke is naturally and necessarily humiliating to all persons, except the one who is on the throne, together with, at most, the one who expects to succeed to it. How different are these cases from that of the power of men over women! I am not now prejudging the question of its justifiableness. I am showing how vastly more permanent it could not but be, even if not justifiable, than these other dominations which have nevertheless lasted down to our own time. Whatever gratification of pride there is in the possession of power, and whatever personal interest in its exercise, is in this case not confined to a limited class, but common to the whole male sex. Instead of being, to most of its supporters, a thing desirable chiefly in the abstract, or, like the political ends usually contended for by factions, of little private importance to any but the leaders; it comes home to the person and hearth of every male head of a family, and of everyone who looks forward to being so. The clodhopper exercises, or is to exercise, his share of the power equally with the highest nobleman. And the case is that in which the desire of power is the strongest: for everyone who desires power, desires it most over those who are nearest to him, with whom his life is passed, with whom he has most concerns in common, and in whom any independence of his authority is oftenest likely to interfere with his individual preferences. If, in the other cases specified, powers manifestly grounded only on force, and having so much less to support them, are so slowly and with so much difficulty got rid of, much more must it be so with this, even if it rests on no better foundation than those. We must consider, too, that the possessors of the power have facilities in this case, greater than in any other, to prevent any uprising against it. Every one of the subjects lives under the very eye, and almost, it may be said, in the hands, of one of the masters— in closer intimacy with him than with any of her fellow-subjects; with no means of combining against him, no power of even locally overmastering him, and, on the other hand, with the strongest motives for seeking his favour and avoiding to give him offence. In struggles for political emancipation, everybody knows how often its champions are bought off by bribes, or daunted by terrors. In the case of women, each individual of the subject-class is in a chronic state of bribery and intimidation combined. In setting up the standard of resistance, a large number of the leaders, and still more of the followers, must make an almost complete sacrifice of the pleasures or the alleviations of their own individual lot. If ever any system of privilege and enforced subjection had its yoke tightly riveted on the necks of those who are kept down by it, this has. I have not yet shown that it is a wrong system: but everyone who is capable of thinking on the subject must see that even if it is, it was certain to outlast all other forms of unjust authority. And when some of the grossest of the other forms still exist in many civilised countries, and have only recently been got rid of in others, it would be strange if that which is so much the deepest rooted had yet been perceptibly shaken anywhere. There is more reason to wonder that the protests and testimonies against it should have been so numerous and so weighty as they are.

Some will object, that a comparison cannot fairly be made between the government of the male sex and the forms of unjust power which I have adduced in illustration of it, since these are arbitrary, and the effect of mere usurpation, while it on the contrary is natural. But was there ever any domination which did not appear natural to those who possessed it? There was a time when the division of mankind into two classes, a small one of masters and a numerous one of slaves, appeared, even to the most cultivated minds, to be natural, and the only natural, condition of the human race. No less an intellect, and one which contributed no less to the progress of human thought, than Aristotle, held this opinion without doubt or misgiving; and rested it on the same premises on which the same assertion in regard to the dominion of men over women is usually based, namely that there are different natures among mankind, free natures, and slave natures; that the Greeks were of a free nature, the barbarian races of Thracians and Asiatics of a slave nature. But why need I go back to Aristotle? Did not the slave-owners of the Southern United States maintain the same doctrine, with all the fanaticism with which men cling to the theories that justify their passions and legitimate their personal interests? Did they not call heaven and earth to witness that the dominion of the white man over the black is natural, that the black race is by nature incapable of freedom, and marked out for slavery? some even going so far as to say that the freedom of manual labourers is an unnatural order of things anywhere. Again, the theorists of absolute monarchy have always affirmed it to be the only natural form of government; issuing from the patriarchal, which was the primitive and spontaneous form of society, framed on the model of the paternal, which is anterior to society itself, and, as they contend, the most natural authority of all. Nay, for that matter, the law of force itself, to those who could not plead any other has always seemed the most natural of all grounds for the exercise of authority. Conquering races hold it to be Nature's own dictate that the conquered should obey the conquerors, or as they euphoniously paraphrase it, that the feebler and more unwarlike races should submit to the braver and manlier. The smallest acquaintance with human life in the middle ages, shows how supremely natural the dominion of the feudal nobility over men of low condition appeared to the nobility themselves, and how unnatural the conception seemed, of a person of the inferior class claiming equality with them, or exercising authority over them. It hardly seemed less so to the class held in subjection. The emancipated serfs and burgesses, even in their most vigorous struggles, never made any pretension to a share of authority; they only demanded more or less of limitation to the power of tyrannising over them. So true is it that unnatural generally means only uncustomary, and that everything which is usual appears natural. The subjection of women to men being a universal custom, any departure from it quite naturally appears unnatural. But how entirely, even in this case, the feeling is dependent on custom, appears by ample experience. Nothing so much astonishes the people of distant parts of the world, when they first learn anything about England, as to be told that it is under a queen; the thing seems to them so unnatural as to be almost incredible. To Englishmen this does not seem in the least degree unnatural, because they are used to it; but they do feel it unnatural that women should be soldiers or Members of Parliament. In the feudal ages, on the contrary, war and politics were not thought unnatural to women, because not unusual; it seemed natural that women of the privileged classes should be of manly character, inferior in nothing but bodily strength to their husbands and fathers. The independence of women seemed rather less unnatural to the Greeks than to other ancients, on account of the fabulous Amazons (whom they believed to be historical), and the partial example afforded by the Spartan women; who, though no less subordinate by law than in other Greek states, were more free in fact, and being trained to bodily exercises in the same manner with men, gave ample proof that they were not naturally disqualified for them. There can be little doubt that Spartan experience suggested to Plato, among many other of his doctrines, that of the social and political equality of the two sexes.

But, it will be said, the rule of men over women differs from all these others in not being a rule of force: it is accepted voluntarily; women make no complaint, and are consenting parties to it. In the first place, a great number of women do not accept it. Ever since there have been women able to make their sentiments known by their writings (the only mode of publicity which society permits to them), an increasing number of them have recorded protests against their present social condition: and recently many thousands of them, headed by the most eminent women known to the public, have petitioned Parliament for their admission to the Parliamentary Suffrage. The claim of women to be educated as solidly, and in the same branches of knowledge, as men, is urged with growing intensity, and with a great prospect of success; while the demand for their admission into professions and occupations hitherto closed against them, becomes every year more urgent. Though there are not in this country, as there are in the United States, periodical conventions and an organised party to agitate for the Rights of Women, there is a numerous and active society organised and managed by women, for the more limited object of obtaining the political franchise. Nor is it only in our own country and in America that women are beginning to protest, more or less collectively, against the disabilities under which they labour. France, and Italy, and Switzerland, and Russia now afford examples of the same thing. How many more women there are who silently cherish similar aspirations, no one can possibly know; but there are abundant tokens how many *would* cherish them, were they not so strenuously taught to repress them as contrary to the proprieties of their sex. It must be remembered, also, that no enslaved class ever asked for complete liberty at once. When Simon de Montfort called the deputies of the commons to sit for the first time in Parliament, did any of them dream of demanding that an assembly, elected by their constituents, should make and destroy ministries, and dictate to the king in affairs of State? No such thought entered into the imagination of the most ambitious. of them. The nobility had already these pretensions; the commons pretended to nothing but to be exempt from arbitrary taxation, and from the gross individual oppression of the king's officers. It is a political law of nature that those who are under any power of ancient origin, never begin by complaining of the power itself, but only of its oppressive exercise. There is never any want of women who complain of ill-usage by their husbands. There would be infinitely more, if complaint were not the greatest of all provocatives to a repetition and increase of the ill-usage. It is this which frustrates all attempts to maintain the power but protect the woman against its abuses. In no other case (except that of a child) is the person who has been proved judicially to have suffered an injury, replaced under the physical power of the culprit who inflicted it. Accordingly wives, even in the most extreme and protracted cases of bodily ill-usage, hardly ever dare avail themselves of the laws made for their protection: and if, in a moment of irrepressible indignation, or by the interference of neighbours, they are induced to do so, their whole effort afterwards is to disclose as little as they can, and to beg off their tyrant from his merited chastisement.

All causes, social and natural, combine to make it unlikely that women should be collectively rebellious to the power of men. They are so far in a position different from all other subject classes, that their masters require something more from them than actual service. Men do not want solely the obedience of women, they want their sentiments. All men, except the most brutish, desire to have, in the woman most nearly connected with them, not a forced slave but a willing one, not a slave merely, but a favourite. They have therefore put everything in practice to enslave their minds. The masters of all other slaves rely, for maintaining obedience, on fear; either fear of themselves, or religious fears. The masters of women wanted more than simple obedience, and they turned the whole force of education to effect their purpose. All women are brought up from the very earliest years in the belief that their ideal of character is the very opposite to that of men; not self-will, and government by self-control, but submission, and yielding to the control of others. All the moralities tell them that it is the duty of women, and all the current sentimentalities that it is their nature, to live for others; to make complete abnegation of themselves, and to have no life but in their affections. And by their affections are meant the only ones they are allowed to have—those to the men with whom they are connected, or to the children who constitute an additional and indefeasible tie between them and a man. When we put together three things—first, the natural attraction between opposite sexes; secondly, the wife's entire dependence on the husband, every privilege or pleasure she has being either his gift, or depending entirely on his will; and lastly, that the principal object of human pursuit, consideration, and all objects of social ambition, can in general be sought or obtained by her only through him, it would be a miracle if the object of being attractive to men had not become the polar star of feminine education and formation of character. And, this great means of influence over the minds of women having been acquired, an instinct of selfishness made men avail themselves of it to the utmost as a means of holding women in subjection, by representing to them meekness, submissiveness, and resignation of all individual will into the hands of a man, as an essential part of sexual attractiveness. Can it be doubted that any of the other yokes which mankind have succeeded in breaking, would have subsisted till now if the same means had existed, and had been so sedulously used, to bow down their minds to it? If it had been made the object of the life of every young plebeian to find personal favour in the eyes of some patrician, of every young serf with some seigneur; if domestication with him, and a share of his personal affections, had been held out as the prize which they all should look out for, the most gifted and aspiring being able to reckon on the most desirable prizes; and if, when this prize had been obtained, they had been shut out by a wall of brass from all interests not centring in him, all feelings and desires but those which he shared or inculcated; would not serfs and seigneurs, plebeians and patricians, have been as broadly distinguished at this day as men and women are? and would not all but a thinker here and there, have believed the distinction to be a fundamental and unalterable fact in human nature?

The preceding considerations are amply sufficient to show that custom, however universal it may be, affords in this case no presumption, and ought not to create any prejudice, in favour of the arrangements which place women in social and political subjection to men. But I may go farther, and maintain that the course of history, and the tendencies of progressive human society, afford not only no presumption in favour of this system of inequality of rights, but a strong one against it; and that, so far as the whole course of human improvement up to the time, the whole stream of modern tendencies, warrants any inference on the subject, it is, that this relic of the past is discordant with the future, and must necessarily disappear.

For, what is the peculiar character of the modern world— the difference which chiefly distinguishes modern institutions, modern social ideas, modern life itself, from those of times long past? It is, that human beings are no longer born to their place in life, and chained down by an inexorable bond to the place they are born to, but are free to employ their faculties, and such favourable chances as offer, to achieve the lot which may appear to them most desirable. Human society of old was constituted on a very different principle. All were born to a fixed social position, and were mostly kept in it by law, or interdicted from any means by which they could emerge from it. As some men are born white and others black, so some were born slaves and others freemen and citizens; some were born patricians, others plebeians; some were born feudal nobles, others commoners and *roturiers*. A slave or serf could never make himself free, nor, except by the will of his master, become so. In most European countries it was not till towards the close of the middle ages, and as a consequence of the growth of regal power, that commoners could be ennobled. Even among nobles, the eldest son was born the exclusive heir to the paternal possessions, and a long time elapsed before it was fully established that the father could disinherit him. Among the industrious classes, only those who were born members of a guild, or were admitted into it by its members, could lawfully practise their calling within its local limits; and nobody could practise any calling deemed important, in any but the legal manner—by processes authoritatively prescribed. Manufacturers have stood in the pillory for presuming to carry on their business by new and improved methods. In modern Europe, and most in those parts of it which have participated most largely in all other modern improvements, diametrically opposite doctrines now prevail. Law and government do not undertake to prescribe by whom any social or industrial operation shall or shall not be conducted, or what modes of conducting them shall be lawful. These things are left to the unfettered choice of individuals. Even the laws which required that workmen should serve an apprenticeship, have in this country been repealed: there being ample assurance that in all cases in which an apprenticeship is necessary, its necessity will suffice to enforce it. The old theory was, that the least possible should be left to the choice of the individual agent; that all he had to do should, as far as practicable, be laid down for him by superior wisdom. Left to himself he was sure to go wrong. The modern conviction, the fruit of a thousand years of experience, is, that things in which the individual is the person directly interested, never go right but as they are left to his own discretion; and that any regulation of them by authority, except to protect the rights of others, is sure to be mischievous. This conclusion, slowly arrived at, and not adopted until almost every possible application of the contrary theory had been made with disastrous result, now (in the industrial department) prevails universally in the most advanced countries, almost universally in all that have pretensions to any sort of advancement. It is not that all processes are supposed to be equally good, or all persons to be equally qualified for everything; but that freedom of individual choice is now known to be the only thing which procures the adoption of the best processes, and throws each operation into the hands of those who are best qualified for it. Nobody thinks it necessary to make a law that only a strong-armed man shall be a blacksmith. Freedom and competition suffice to make blacksmiths strong-armed men, because the weak-armed can earn more by engaging in occupations for which they are more fit. In consonance with this doctrine, it is felt to be an overstepping of the proper bounds of authority to fix beforehand, on some general presumption, that certain persons are not fit to do certain things. It is now thoroughly known and admitted that if some such presumptions exist, no such presumption is infallible. Even if it be well grounded in a majority of cases, which it is very likely not to be, there will be a minority of exceptional cases in which it does not hold: and in those it is both an injustice to the individuals, and a detriment to society, to place barriers in the way of their using their faculties for their own benefit and for that of others. In the cases, on the other hand, in which the unfitness is real, the ordinary motives of human conduct will on the whole suffice to prevent the incompetent person from making, or from persisting in, the attempt.

If this general principle of social and economical science is not true; if individuals, with such help as they can derive from the opinion of those who know them, are not better judges than the law and the government, of their own capacities and vocation; the world cannot too soon abandon this principle, and return to the old system of regulations and disabilities. But if the principle is true, we ought to act as if we believed it, and not to ordain that to be born a girl instead of a boy, any more than to be born black instead of white, or a commoner instead of a nobleman, shall decide the person's position through all life—shall interdict people from all the more elevated social positions, and from all, except a few, respectable occupations. Even were we to admit the utmost that is ever pretended as to the superior fitness of men for all the functions now reserved to them, the same argument applies which forbids a legal qualification for Members of Parliament. If only once in a dozen years the conditions of eligibility exclude a fit person, there is a real loss, while the exclusion of thousands of unfit persons is no gain; for if the constitution of the electoral body disposes them to choose unfit persons, there are always plenty of such persons to choose from. In all things of any difficulty and importance, those who can do them well are fewer than the need, even with the most unrestricted latitude of choice: and any limitation of the field of selection deprives society of some chances of being served by the competent, without ever saving it from the incompetent.

At present, in the more improved countries, the disabilities of women are the only case, save one, in which laws and institutions take persons at their birth, and ordain that they shall never in all their lives be allowed to compete for certain things. The one exception is that of royalty. Persons still are born to the throne; no one, not of the reigning family, can ever occupy it, and no one even of that family can, by any means but the course of hereditary succession, attain it. All other dignities and social advantages are open to the whole male sex: many indeed are only attainable by wealth, but wealth may be striven for by anyone, and is actually obtained by many men of the very humblest origin. The difficulties, to the majority, are indeed insuperable without the aid of fortunate accidents; but no male human being is under any legal ban: neither law nor opinion superadd artificial obstacles to the natural ones. Royalty, as I have said, is excepted: but in this case every-one feels it to be an exception—an anomaly in the modern world, in marked opposition to its customs and principles, and to be justified only by extraordinary special expediences, which, though individuals and nations differ in estimating their weight, unquestionably do in fact exist. But in this exceptional case, in which a high social function is, for important reasons, bestowed on birth instead of being put up to competition, all free nations contrive to adhere in substance to the principle from which they nominally derogate; for they circumscribe this high function by conditions avowedly intended to prevent the person to whom it ostensibly belongs from really performing it; while the person by whom it is performed, the responsible minister, does obtain the post by a competition from which no full-grown citizen of the male sex is legally excluded. The disabilities, therefore, to which women are subject from the mere fact of their birth, are the solitary examples of the kind in modern legislation. In no instance except this, which comprehends half the human race, are the higher social functions closed against anyone by a fatality of birth which no exertions, and no change of circumstances, can overcome; for even religious disabilities (besides that in England and in Europe they have practically almost ceased to exist) do not close any career to the disqualified person in case of conversion.

The social subordination of women thus stands out an isolated fact in modern social institutions; a solitary breach of what has become their fundamental law; a single relic of an old world of thought and practice exploded in everything else, but retained in the one thing of most universal interest; as if a gigantic dolmen, or a vast temple of Jupiter Olympius, occupied the site of St. Paul's and received daily worship, while the surrounding Christian churches were only resorted to on fasts and festivals. This entire discrepancy between one social fact and all those which accompany it, and the radical opposition between its nature and the progressive movement which is the boast of the modern world, and which has successively swept away everything else of an analogous character, surely affords, to a conscientious observer of human tendencies, serious matter for reflection. It raises a prima facie presumption on the unfavourable side, far outweighing any which custom and usage could in such circumstances create on the favourable; and should at least suffice to make this, like the choice between republicanism and royalty, a balanced question.

The least that can be demanded is, that the question should not be considered as prejudged by existing fact and existing opinion, but open to discussion on its merits, as a question of justice and expediency: the decision on this, as on any of the other social arrangements of mankind, depending on what an enlightened estimate of tendencies and consequences may show to be most advantageous to humanity in general, without distinction of sex. And the discussion must be a real discussion, descending to foundations, and not resting satisfied with vague and general assertions. It will not do, for instance, to assert in general terms, that the experience of mankind has pronounced in favour of the existing system. Experience cannot possibly have decided between two courses, so long as there has only been experience of one. If it be said that the doctrine of the equality of the sexes rests only on theory, it must be remembered that the contrary doctrine also has only theory to rest upon. All that is proved in its favour by direct experience, is that mankind have been able to exist under it, and to attain the degree of improvement and prosperity which we now see; but whether that prosperity has been attained sooner, or is now greater, than it would have been under the other system, experience does not say. On the other hand, experience does say, that every step in improvement has been so invariably accompanied by a step made in raising the social position of women, that historians and philosophers have been led to adopt their elevation or debasement as on the whole the surest test and most correct measure of the civilisation of a people or an age. Through all the progressive period of human history, the condition of women has been approaching nearer to equality with men. This does not of itself prove that the assimilation must go on to complete equality; but it assuredly affords some presumption that such is the case.

Neither does it avail anything to say that the *nature* of the two sexes adapts them to their present functions and position, and renders these appropriate to them. Standing on the ground of common sense and the constitution of the human mind, I deny that anyone knows, or can know, the nature of the two sexes, as long as they have only been seen in their present relation to one another. If men had ever been found in society without women, or women without men, or if there had been a society of men and women in which the women were not under the control of the men, something might have been positively known about the mental and moral differences which may be inherent in the nature of each. What is now called the nature of women is an eminently artificial thing—the result of forced repression in some directions, unnatural stimulation in others. It may be asserted without scruple, that no other class of dependents have had their character so entirely distorted from its natural proportions by their relation with their masters; for, if conquered and slave races have been, in some respects, more forcibly repressed, whatever in them has not been crushed down by an iron heel has generally been let alone, and if left with any liberty of development, it has developed itself according to its own laws; but in the case of women, a hot-house and stove cultivation has always been carried on of some of the capabilities of their nature, for the benefit and pleasure of their masters. Then, because certain products of the general vital force sprout luxuriantly and reach a great development in this heated atmosphere and under this active nurture and watering, while other shoots from the same root, which are left outside in the wintry air, with ice purposely heaped all round them, have a stunted growth, and some are burnt off with fire and disappear; men, with that inability to recognise their own work which distinguishes the unanalytic mind, indolently believe that the tree grows of itself in the way they have made it grow, and that it would die if one half of it were not kept in a vapour bath and the other half in the snow.

Of all difficulties which impede the progress of thought, and the formation of well-grounded opinions on life and social arrangements, the greatest is now the unspeakable ignorance and inattention of mankind in respect to the influences which form human character. Whatever any portion of the human species now are, or seem to be, such, it is supposed, they have a natural tendency to be: even when the most elementary knowledge of the circumstances in which they have been placed, clearly points out the causes that made them what they are. Because a cottier deeply in arrears to his landlord is not industrious, there are people who think that the Irish are naturally idle. Because constitutions can be overthrown when the authorities appointed to execute them turn their arms against them, there are people who think the French incapable of free government. Because the Greeks cheated the Turks, and the Turks only plundered the Greeks, there are persons who think that the Turks are naturally more sincere: and because women, as is often said, care nothing about politics except their personalities, it is supposed that the general good is naturally less interesting to women than to men. History, which is now so much better understood than formerly, teaches another lesson: if only by showing the extraordinary susceptibility of human nature to external influences, and the extreme variableness of those of its manifestations which are supposed to be most universal and uniform. But in history, as in travelling, men usually see only what they already had in their own minds; and few learn much from history, who do not bring much with them to its study.

Hence, in regard to that most difficult question, what are the natural differences between the two sexes—a subject on which it is impossible in the present state of society to obtain complete and correct knowledge—while almost everybody dogmatises upon it, almost all neglect and make light of the only means by which any partial insight can be obtained into it. This is, an analytic study of the most important department of psychology, the laws of the influence of circumstances on character. For, however great and apparently ineradicable the moral and intellectual differences between men and women might be, the evidence of there being natural differences could only be negative. Those only could be inferred to be natural which could not possibly be artificial—the residuum, after deducting every characteristic of either sex which can admit of being explained from education or external circumstances. The profoundest knowledge of the laws of the formation of character is indispensable to entitle anyone to affirm even that there is any difference, much more what the difference is, between the two sexes considered as moral and rational beings; and since no one, as yet, has that knowledge (for there is hardly any subject which, in proportion to its importance, has been so little studied), no one is thus far entitled to any positive opinion on the subject. Conjectures are all that can at present be made; conjectures more or less probable, according as more or less authorised by such knowledge as we yet have of the laws of psychology, as applied to the formation of character.

Even the preliminary knowledge, what the differences between the sexes now are, apart from all question as to how they are made what they are, is still in the crudest and most incomplete state. Medical practitioners and physiologists have ascertained, to some extent, the differences in bodily constitution; and this is an important element to the psychologist: but hardly any medical practitioner is a psychologist. Respecting the mental characteristics of women; their observations are of no more worth than those of common men. It is a subject on which nothing final can be known, so long as those who alone can really know it, women themselves, have given but little testimony, and that little, mostly suborned. It is easy to know stupid women. Stupidity is much the same all the world over. A stupid person's notions and feelings may confidently be inferred from those which prevail in the circle by which the person is surrounded. Not so with those whose opinions and feelings are an emanation from their own nature and faculties. It is only a man here and there who has any tolerable knowledge of the character even of the women of his own family. I do not mean, of their capabilities; these nobody knows, not even themselves, because most of them have never been called out. I mean their actually existing thoughts and feelings. Many a man thinks he perfectly understands women, because he has had amatory relations with several, perhaps with many of them.

If he is a good observer, and his experience extends to quality as well as quantity, he may have learnt something of one narrow department of their nature—an important department, no doubt. But of all the rest of it, few persons are generally more ignorant, because there are few from whom it is so carefully hidden. The most favourable case which a man can generally have for studying the character of a woman, is that of his own wife: for the opportunities are greater, and the cases of complete sympathy not so unspeakably rare. And in fact, this is the source from which any knowledge worth having on the subject has, I believe, generally come. But most men have not had the opportunity of studying in this way more than a single case: accordingly one can, to an almost laughable degree, infer what a man's wife is like, from his opinions about women in general. To make even this one case yield any result, the woman must be worth knowing, and the man not only a competent judge, but of a character so sympathetic in itself, and so well adapted to hers, that he can either read her mind by sympathetic intuition, or has nothing in himself which makes her shy of disclosing it. Hardly anything, I believe, can be more rare than this conjunction. It often happens that there is the most complete unity of feeling and community of interests as to all external things, yet the one has as little admission into the internal life of the other as if they were common acquaintance. Even with true affection, authority on the one side and subordination on the other prevent perfect confidence. Though nothing may be intentionally withheld, much is not shown. In the analogous relation of parent and child, the corresponding phenomenon must have been in the observation of everyone. As between father and son, how many are the cases in which the father, in spite of real affection on both sides, obviously to all the world does not know, nor suspect, parts of the son's character familiar to his companions and equals. The truth is, that the position of looking up to another is extremely unpropitious to complete sincerity and openness with him. The fear of losing ground in his opinion or in his feelings is so strong, that even in an upright character, there is an unconscious tendency to show only the best side, or the side which, though not the best, is that which he most likes to see: and it may be confidently said that thorough knowledge of one another hardly ever exists, but between persons who, besides being intimates, are equals. How much more true, then, must all this be, when the one is not only under the authority of the other, but has it inculcated on her as a duty to reckon everything else subordinate to his comfort and pleasure, and to let him neither see nor feel anything coming from her, except what is agreeable to him. All these difficulties stand in the way of a man's obtaining any thorough knowledge even of the one woman whom alone, in general, he has sufficient opportunity of studying. When we further consider that to understand one woman is not necessarily to understand any other woman; that even if he could study many women of one rank, or of one country, he would not thereby understand women of other ranks or countries; and even if he did, they are still only the women of a single period of history; we may safely assert that the knowledge which men can acquire of women, even as they have been and are, without reference to what they might be, is wretchedly imperfect and superficial, and always will be so, until women themselves have told all that they have to tell.

And this time has not come; nor will it come otherwise than gradually. It is but of yesterday that women have either been qualified by literary accomplishments, or permitted by society, to tell anything to the general public. As yet very few of them dare tell anything, which men, on whom their literary success depends, are unwilling to hear. Let us remember in what manner, up to a very recent time, the expression, even by a male author, of uncustomary opinions, or what are deemed eccentric feelings, usually was, and in some degree still is, received; and we may form some faint conception under what impediments a woman, who is brought up to think custom and opinion her sovereign rule, attempts to express in books anything drawn from the depths of her own nature. The greatest woman who has left writings behind her sufficient to give her an eminent rank in the literature of her country, thought it necessary to prefix as a motto to her boldest work, "Un homme peut braver l'opinion; une femme doit s'y soumettre." [1] The greater part of what women write about women is mere sycophancy to men. In the case of unmarried women, much of it seems only intended to increase their chance of a husband. Many, both married and unmarried, overstep the mark, and inculcate a servility beyond what is desired or relished by any man, except the very vulgarest. But this is not so often the case as, even at a quite late period, it still was. Literary women are becoming more free-spoken, and more willing to express their

[1] Title-page of Mme de Staël's *Delphine.*

real sentiments. Unfortunately, in this country especially, they are themselves such artificial products, that their sentiments are compounded of a small element of individual observation and consciousness, and a very large one of acquired associations. This will be less and less the case, but it will remain true to a great extent, as long as social institutions do not admit the same free development of originality in women which is possible to men. When that time comes, and not before, we shall see, and not merely hear, as much as it is necessary to know of the nature of women, and the adaptation of other things to it.

I have dwelt so much on the difficulties which at present obstruct any real knowledge by men of the true nature of women, because in this as in so many other things "opinio copiæ inter maximas causas inopiæ est"; and there is little chance of reasonable thinking on the matter, while people flatter themselves that they perfectly understand a subject of which most men know absolutely nothing, and of which it is at present impossible that any man, or all men taken together, should have knowledge which can qualify them to lay down the law to women as to what is, or is not, their vocation. Happily, no such knowledge is necessary for any practical purpose connected with the position of women in relation to society and life. For, according to all the principles involved in modern society, the question rests with women themselves—to be decided by their own experience, and by the use of their own faculties. There are no means of finding what either one person or many can do, but by trying—and no means by which anyone else can discover for them what it is for their happiness to do or leave undone.

One thing we may be certain of—that what is contrary to women's nature to do, they never will be made to do by simply giving their nature free play. The anxiety of mankind to interfere in behalf of nature, for fear lest nature should not succeed in effecting its purpose, is an altogether unnecessary solicitude. What women by nature cannot do, it is quite superfluous to forbid them from doing. What they can do, but not so well as the men who are their competitors, competition suffices to exclude them from; since nobody asks for protective duties and bounties in favour of women; it is only asked that the present bounties and protective duties in favour of men should be recalled. If women have a greater natural inclination for some things than for others, there is no need of laws or social inculcation to make the majority of them do the former in preference to the latter.   Whatever women's services are most wanted for, the free play of competition will hold out the strongest inducements to them to undertake.   And, as the words imply, they are most wanted for the things for which they are most fit; by the apportionment of which to them, the collective faculties of the two sexes can be applied on the whole with the greatest sum of valuable result.

The general opinion of men is supposed to be, that the natural vocation of a woman is that of a wife and mother.   I say, is supposed to be, because, judging from acts—from the whole of the present constitution of society—one might infer that their opinion was the direct contrary.   They might be supposed to think that the alleged natural vocation of women was of all things the most repugnant to their nature; insomuch that if they are free to do anything else—if any other means of living or occupation of their time and faculties, is open, which has any chance of appearing desirable to them—there will not be enough of them who will be willing to accept the condition said to be natural to them.   If this is the real opinion of men in general, it would be well that it should be spoken out.   I should like to hear somebody openly enunciating the doctrine (it is already implied in much that is written on the subject)—"It is necessary to society that women should marry and produce children.   They will not do so unless they are compelled.   Therefore it is necessary to compel them."   The merits of the case would then be clearly defined.   It would be exactly that of the slave-holders of South Carolina and Louisiana.   "It is necessary that cotton and sugar should be grown.   White men cannot produce them.   Negroes will not, for any wages which we choose to give.   *Ergo* they must be compelled."   An illustration still closer to the point is that of impressment.   Sailors must absolutely be had to defend the country.   It often happens that they will not voluntarily enlist.   Therefore there must be the power of forcing them.   How often has this logic been used! and, but for one flaw in it, without doubt it would have been successful up to this day.   But it is open to the retort—First pay the sailors the honest value of their labour.   When you have made it as well worth their while to serve you, as to work for other employers, you will have no more difficulty than others have in obtaining their services.   To this there is no logical answer except "I will not": and as people are now not only ashamed, but are not desirous, to rob the labourer of his hire, impressment is no longer advocated. Those who attempt to force women into marriage by closing all other doors against them, lay themselves open to a similar retort. If they mean what they say, their opinion must evidently be, that men do not render the married condition so desirable to women, as to induce them to accept it for its own recommendations. It is not a sign of one's thinking the boon one offers very attractive, when one allows only Hobson's choice, "that or none." And here, I believe, is the clue to the feelings of those men, who have a real antipathy to the equal freedom of women. I believe they are afraid, not lest women should be unwilling to marry, for I do not think that anyone in reality has that apprehension; but lest they should insist that marriage should be on equal conditions; lest all women of spirit and capacity should prefer doing almost anything else, not in their own eyes degrading, rather than marry, when marrying is giving themselves a master, and a master too of all their earthly possessions. And truly, if this consequence were necessarily incident to marriage, I think that the apprehension would be very well founded. I agree in thinking it probable that few women, capable of anything else, would, unless under an irresistible *entrainement*, rendering them for the time insensible to anything but itself, choose such a lot, when any other means were open to them of filling a conventionally honourable place in life: and if men are determined that the law of marriage shall be a law of despotism, they are quite right, in point of mere policy, in leaving to women only Hobson's choice. But, in that case, all that has been done in the modern world to relax the chain on the minds of women, has been a mistake. They never should have been allowed to receive a literary education. Women who read, much more women who write, are, in the existing constitution of things, a contradiction and a disturbing element: and it was wrong to bring women up with any acquirements but those of an odalisque, or of a domestic servant.

CHAPTER II

IT will be well to commence the detailed discussion of the subject by the particular branch of it to which the course of our observations has led us: the conditions which the laws of this and all other countries annex to the marriage contract. Marriage being the destination appointed by society for women, the prospect they are brought up to, and the object which it is intended should be sought by all of them, except those who are too little attractive to be chosen by any man as his companion; one might have supposed that everything would have been done to make this condition as eligible to them as possible, that they might have no cause to regret being denied the option of any other. Society, however, both in this, and, at first, in all other cases, has preferred to attain its object by foul rather than fair means: but this is the only case in which it has substantially persisted in them even to the present day. Originally women were taken by force, or regularly sold by their father to the husband. Until a late period in European history, the father had the power to dispose of his daughter in marriage at his own will and pleasure, without any regard to hers. The Church, indeed, was so far faithful to a better morality as to require a formal "yes" from the woman at the marriage ceremony; but there was nothing to show that the consent was other than compulsory; and it was practically impossible for the girl to refuse compliance if the father persevered, except perhaps when she might obtain the protection of religion by a determined resolution to take monastic vows. After marriage, the man had anciently (but this was anterior to Christianity) the power of life and death over his wife. She could invoke no law against him; he was her sole tribunal and law. For a long time he could repudiate her, but she had no corresponding power in regard to him. By the old laws of England, the husband was called the *lord* of the wife; he was literally regarded as her sovereign, inasmuch that the murder of a man by his wife was called treason (*petty* as distinguished from *high* treason), and was more cruelly avenged than was usually the case with high treason, for the penalty was burning to death. Because these

various enormities have fallen into disuse (for most of them
were never formally abolished, or not until they had long
ceased to be practised) men suppose that all is now as it should
be in regard to the marriage contract; and we are continually
told that civilisation and Christianity have restored to the
woman her just rights.   Meanwhile the wife is the actual bond-
servant of her husband: no less so, as far as legal obligation
goes, than slaves commonly so called.   She vows a livelong
obedience to him at the altar, and is held to it all through her
life by law.   Casuists may say that the obligation of obedience
stops short of participation in crime, but it certainly extends
to everything else.   She can do no act whatever but by his
permission, at least tacit.   She can acquire no property but
for him; the instant it becomes hers, even if by inheritance, it
becomes *ipso facto* his.   In this respect the wife's position under
the common law of England is worse than that of slaves in the
laws of many countries: by the Roman law, for example, a
slave might have his peculium, which to a certain extent the
law guaranteed to him for his exclusive use.   The higher classes
in this country have given an analogous advantage to their
women, through special contracts setting aside the law, by
conditions of pin-money, etc.: since parental feeling being
stronger with fathers than the class feeling of their own sex,
a father generally prefers his own daughter to a son-in-law who
is a stranger to him.   By means of settlements, the rich usually
contrive to withdraw the whole or part of the inherited property
of the wife from the absolute control of the husband: but they
do not succeed in keeping it under her own control; the utmost
they can do only prevents the husband from squandering it,
at the same time debarring the rightful owner from its use.
The property itself is out of the reach of both; and as to the
income derived from it, the form of settlement most favourable
to the wife (that called "to her separate use") only precludes
the husband from receiving it instead of her: it must pass
through her hands, but if he takes it from her by personal
violence as soon as she receives it, he can neither be punished,
nor compelled to restitution.   This is the amount of the protection which, under the laws of this country, the most powerful
nobleman can give to his own daughter as respects her husband.
In the immense majority of cases there is no settlement: and
the absorption of all rights, all property, as well as all freedom
of action, is complete.   The two are called "one person in
law," for the purpose of inferring that whatever is hers is his,

but the parallel inference is never drawn that whatever is his is hers; the maxim is not applied against the man, except to make him responsible to third parties for her acts, as a master is for the acts of his slaves or of his cattle.   I am far from pretending that wives are in general no better treated than slaves; but no slave is a slave to the same lengths, and in so full a sense of the word, as a wife is.   Hardly any slave, except one immediately attached to the master's person, is a slave at all hours and all minutes; in general he has, like a soldier, his fixed task, and when it is done, or when he is off duty, he disposes, within certain limits, of his own time, and has a family life into which the master rarely intrudes.   "Uncle Tom" under his first master had his own life in his "cabin," almost as much as any man whose work takes him away from home, is able to have in his own family.   But it cannot be so with the wife. Above all, a female slave has (in Christian countries) an admitted right, and is considered under a moral obligation, to refuse to her master the last familiarity.   Not so the wife: however brutal a tyrant she may unfortunately be chained to—though she may know that he hates her, though it may be his daily pleasure to torture her, and though she may feel it impossible not to loathe him—he can claim from her and enforce the lowest degradation of a human being, that of being made the instrument of an animal function contrary to her inclinations. While she is held in this worst description of slavery as to her own person, what is her position in regard to the children in whom she and her master have a joint interest?   They are by law *his* children.   He alone has any legal rights over them. Not one act can she do towards or in relation to them, except by delegation from him.   Even after he is dead she is not their legal guardian, unless he by will has made her so.   He could even send them away from her, and deprive her of the means of seeing or corresponding with them, until this power was in some degree restricted by Serjeant Talfourd's Act.   This is her legal state.   And from this state she has no means of withdrawing herself.   If she leaves her husband, she can take nothing with her, neither her children nor anything which is rightfully her own.   If he chooses, he can compel her to return, by law, or by physical force; or he may content himself with seizing for his own use anything which she may earn, or which may be given to her by her relations.   It is only legal separation by a decree of a court of justice, which entitles her to live apart, without being forced back into the custody of an exasperated

jailer—or which empowers her to apply any earnings to her
own use, without fear that a man whom perhaps she has not
seen for twenty years will pounce upon her some day and carry
all off.   This legal separation, until lately, the courts of justice
would only give at an expense which made it inaccessible to
anyone out of the higher ranks.   Even now it is only given in
cases of desertion, or of the extreme of cruelty; and yet complaints are made every day that it is granted too easily.   Surely,
if a woman is denied any lot in life but that of being the personal
body-servant of a despot, and is dependent for everything upon
the chance of finding one who may be disposed to make a
favourite of her instead of merely a drudge, it is a very cruel
aggravation of her fate that she should be allowed to try this
chance only once.   The natural sequel and corollary from this
state of things would be, that since her all in life depends upon
obtaining a good master, she should be allowed to change again
and again until she finds one.   I am not saying that she ought
to be allowed this privilege.   That is a totally different consideration.   The question of divorce, in the sense involving
liberty of remarriage, is one into which it is foreign to my
purpose to enter.   All I now say is, that to those to whom
nothing but servitude is allowed, the free choice of servitude
is the only, though a most insufficient, alleviation.   Its refusal
completes the assimilation of the wife to the slave—and the
slave under not the mildest form of slavery: for in some slave
codes the slave could, under certain circumstances of ill usage,
legally compel the master to sell him.   But no amount of ill
usage, without adultery superadded, will in England free a
wife from her tormentor.

I have no desire to exaggerate, nor does the case stand in
any need of exaggeration.   I have described the wife's legal
position, not her actual treatment.   The laws of most countries
are far worse than the people who execute them, and many of
them are only able to remain laws by being seldom or never
carried into effect.   If married life were all that it might be expected to be, looking to the laws alone, society would be a
hell upon earth.   Happily there are both feelings and interests
which in many men exclude, and in most, greatly temper, the
impulses and propensities which lead to tyranny: and of those
feelings, the tie which connects a man with his wife affords, in
a normal state of things, incomparably the strongest example.
The only tie which at all approaches to it, that between him and
his children, tends, in all save exceptional cases, to strengthen,

instead of conflicting with, the first. Because this is true; because men in general do not inflict, nor women suffer, all the misery which could be inflicted and suffered if the full power of tyranny with which the man is legally invested were acted on; the defenders of the existing form of the institution think that all its iniquity is justified, and that any complaint is merely quarrelling with the evil which is the price paid for every great good. But the mitigations in practice, which are compatible with maintaining in full legal force this or any other kind of tyranny, instead of being any apology for despotism, only serve to prove what power human nature possesses of reacting against the vilest institutions, and with what vitality the seeds of good as well as those of evil in human character diffuse and propagate themselves. Not a word can be said for despotism in the family which cannot be said for political despotism. Every absolute king does not sit at his window to enjoy the groans of his tortured subjects, nor strips them of their last rag and turns them out to shiver in the road. The despotism of Louis XVI was not the despotism of Philippe le Bel, or of Nadir Shah, or of Caligula; but it was bad enough to justify the French Revolution, and to palliate even its horrors. If an appeal be made to the intense attachments which exist between wives and their husbands, exactly as much may be said of domestic slavery. It was quite an ordinary fact in Greece and Rome for slaves to submit to death by torture rather than betray their masters. In the proscriptions of the Roman civil wars it was remarked that wives and slaves were heroically faithful, sons very commonly treacherous. Yet we know how cruelly many Romans treated their slaves. But in truth these intense individual feelings nowhere rise to such a luxuriant height as under the most atrocious institutions. It is part of the irony of life, that the strongest feelings of devoted gratitude of which human nature seems to be susceptible, are called forth in human beings towards those who, having the power entirely to crush their earthly existence, voluntarily refrain from using that power. How great a place in most men this sentiment fills, even in religious devotion, it would be cruel to inquire. We daily see how much their gratitude to Heaven appears to be stimulated by the contemplation of fellow-creatures to whom God has not been so merciful as he has to themselves.

Whether the institution to be defended is slavery, political absolutism, or the absolutism of the head of a family, we are always expected to judge of it from its best instances; and we are presented with pictures of loving exercise of authority on one side, loving submission to it on the other—superior wisdom ordering all things for the greatest good of the dependents, and surrounded by their smiles and benedictions. All this would be very much to the purpose if anyone pretended that there are no such things as good men. Who, doubts that there may be great goodness, and great happiness, and great affection, under the absolute government of a good man? Meanwhile, laws and institutions require to be adapted, not to good men, but to bad. Marriage is not an institution designed for a select few. Men are not required, as a preliminary to the marriage ceremony, to prove by testimonials that they are fit to be trusted with the exercise of absolute power. The tie of affection and obligation to a wife and children is very strong with those whose general social feelings are strong, and with many who are little sensible to any other social ties; but there are all degrees of sensibility and insensibility to it, as there are all grades of goodness and wickedness in men, down to those whom no ties will bind, and on whom society has no action but through its *ultima ratio*, the penalties of the law. In every grade of this descending scale are men to whom are committed all the legal powers of a husband. The vilest malefactor has some wretched woman tied to him, against whom he can commit any atrocity except killing her, and, if tolerably cautious, can do that without much danger of the legal penalty. And how many thousands are there among the lowest classes in every country, who, without being in a legal sense malefactors in any other respect, because in every other quarter their aggressions meet with resistance, indulge the utmost habitual excesses of bodily violence towards the unhappy wife, who alone, at least of grown persons, can neither repel nor escape from their brutality; and towards whom the excess of dependence inspires their mean and savage natures, not with a generous forbearance, and a point of honour to behave well to one whose lot in life is trusted entirely to their kindness, but on the contrary with a notion that the law has delivered her to them as their thing, to be used at their pleasure, and that they are not expected to practise the consideration towards her which is required from them towards everybody else. The law, which till lately left even these atrocious extremes of domestic oppression practically unpunished, has within these few years made some feeble attempts to repress them. But its attempts have done little, and cannot be expected to do much, because it is contrary to reason and experience to suppose that there can be any real check to brutality, consistent with leaving the victim still in the power of the executioner. Until a conviction for personal violence, or at all events a repetition of it after a first conviction, entitles the woman *ipso facto* to a divorce, or at least to a judicial separation, the attempt to repress these "aggravated assaults" by legal penalties will break down for want of a prosecutor, or for want of a witness.

When we consider how vast is the number of men, in any great country, who are little higher than brutes, and that this never prevents them from being able, through the law of marriage, to obtain a victim, the breadth and depth of human misery caused in this shape alone by the abuse of the institution swells to something appalling. Yet these are only the extreme cases. They are the lowest abysses, but there is a sad succession of depth after depth before reaching them. In domestic as in political tyranny, the case of absolute monsters chiefly illustrates the institution by showing that there is scarcely any horror which may not occur under it if the despot pleases, and thus setting in a strong light what must be the terrible frequency of things only a little less atrocious. Absolute fiends are as rare as angels, perhaps rarer: ferocious savages, with occasional touches of humanity, are however very frequent: and in the wide interval which separates these from any worthy representatives of the human species, how many are the forms and gradations of animalism and selfishness, often under an outward varnish of civilisation and even cultivation, living at peace with the law, maintaining a creditable appearance to all who are not under their power, yet sufficient often to make the lives of all who are so, a torment and a burthen to them! It would be tiresome to repeat the commonplaces about the unfitness of men in general for power, which, after the political discussions of centuries, everyone knows by heart, were it not that hardly anyone thinks of applying these maxims to the case in which above all others they are applicable, that of power, not placed in the hands of a man here and there, but offered to every adult male, down to the basest and most ferocious. It is not because a man is not known to have broken any of the Ten Commandments, or because he maintains a respectable character in his dealings with those whom he cannot compel to have intercourse with him, or because he does not fly out into violent bursts of ill-temper against those who are not obliged to bear with him, that it is possible to surmise of what sort his conduct

will be in the unrestraint of home. Even the commonest men
reserve the violent, the sulky, the undisguisedly selfish side of
their character for those who have no power to withstand it.
The relation of superiors to dependents is the nursery of these
vices of character, which, wherever else they exist, are an over-
flowing from that source. A man who is morose or violent to
his equals, is sure to be one who has lived among inferiors,
whom he could frighten or worry into submission. If the
family in its best forms is, as it is often said to be, a school of
sympathy, tenderness, and loving forgetfulness of self, it is still
oftener, as respects its chief, a school of wilfulness, overbearingness, unbounded selfish indulgence, and a double - dyed and
idealised selfishness, of which sacrifice itself is only a particular
form: the care for the wife and children being only care for
them as parts of the man's own interests and belongings, and
their individual happiness being immolated in every shape to
his smallest preferences. What better is to be looked for under
the existing form of the institution? We know that the bad
propensities of human nature are only kept within bounds
when they are allowed no scope for their indulgence. We
know that from impulse and habit, when not from deliberate
purpose, almost everyone to whom others yield, goes on en-
croaching upon them, until a point is reached at which they
are compelled to resist. Such being the common tendency of
human nature; the almost unlimited power which present social
institutions give to the man over at least one human being—
the one with whom he resides, and whom he has always present
—this power seeks out and evokes the latent germs of selfishness in the remotest corners of his nature—fans its faintest
sparks and smouldering embers—offers to him a licence for the
indulgence of those points of his original character which in all
other relations he would have found it necessary to repress and
conceal, and the repression of which would in time have become
a second nature. I know that there is another side to the
question. I grant that the wife, if she cannot effectually resist,
can at least retaliate; she, too, can make the man's life extremely
uncomfortable, and by that power is able to carry many points
which she ought, and many which she ought not, to prevail in.
But this instrument of self-protection—which may be called
the power of the scold, or the shrewish sanction—has the fatal
defect, that it avails most against the least tyrannical superiors,
and in favour of the least deserving dependents. It is the
weapon of irritable and self-willed women; of those who would

make the worst use of power if they themselves had it, and who generally turn this power to a bad use. The amiable cannot use such an instrument, the highminded disdain it. And on the other hand, the husbands against whom it is used most effectively are the gentler and more inoffensive; those who cannot be induced, even by provocation, to resort to any very harsh exercise of authority. The wife's power of being disagreeable generally only establishes a counter-tyranny, and makes victims in their turn chiefly of those husbands who are least inclined to be tyrants.

What is it, then, which really tempers the corrupting effects of the power, and makes it compatible with such amount of good as we actually see? Mere feminine blandishments, though of great effect in individual instances, have very little effect in modifying the general tendencies of the situation; for their power only lasts while the woman is young and attractive, often only while her charm is new, and not dimmed by familiarity; and on many men they have not much influence at any time. The real mitigating causes are, the personal affection which is the growth of time in so far as the man's nature is susceptible of it and the woman's character sufficiently congenial with his to excite it; their common interests as regards the children, and their general community of interest as concerns third persons (to which however there are very great limitations); the real importance of the wife to his daily comforts and enjoyments, and the value he consequently attaches to her on his personal account, which, in a man capable of feeling for others, lays the foundation of caring for her on her own; and lastly, the influence naturally acquired over almost all human beings by those near to their persons (if not actually disagreeable to them): who, both by their direct entreaties, and by the insensible contagion of their feelings and dispositions, are often able, unless counteracted by some equally strong personal influence, to obtain a degree of command over the conduct of the superior, altogether excessive and unreasonable. Through these various means, the wife frequently exercises even too much power over the man; she is able to affect his conduct in things in which she may not be qualified to influence it for good—in which her influence may be not only unenlightened, but employed on the morally wrong side; and in which he would act better if left to his own prompting. But neither in the affairs of families nor in those of states is power a compensation for the loss of freedom. Her power often gives her what she has no right to, but does not enable her to assert her own rights. A Sultan's favourite slave has slaves under her, over whom she tyrannises; but the desirable thing would be that she should neither have slaves nor be a slave. By entirely sinking her own existence in her husband; by having no will (or persuading him that she has no will) but his, in anything which regards their joint relation, and by making it the business of her life to work upon his sentiments, a wife may gratify herself by influencing, and very probably perverting, his conduct, in those of his external relations which she has never qualified herself to judge of, or in which she is herself wholly influenced by some personal or other partiality or prejudice. Accordingly, as things now are, those who act most kindly to their wives, are quite as often made worse, as better, by the wife's influence, in respect to all interests extending beyond the family. She is taught that she has no business with things out of that sphere; and accordingly she seldom has any honest and conscientious opinion on them; and therefore hardly ever meddles with them for any legitimate purpose, but generally for an interested one. She neither knows nor cares which is the right side in politics, but she knows what will bring in money or invitations, give her husband a title, her son a place, or her daughter a good marriage.

But how, it will be asked, can any society exist without government? In a family, as in a state, some one person must be the ultimate ruler. Who shall decide when married people differ in opinion? Both cannot have their way, yet a decision one way or the other must be come to.

It is not true that in all voluntary association between two people, one of them must be absolute master: still less that the law must determine which of them it shall be. The most frequent case of voluntary association, next to marriage, is partnership in business: and it is not found or thought necessary to enact that in every partnership, one partner shall have entire control over the concern, and the others shall be bound to obey his orders. No one would enter into partnership on terms which would subject him to the responsibilities of a principal, with only the powers and privileges of a clerk or agent. If the law dealt with other contracts as it does with marriage, it would ordain that one partner should administer the common business as if it was his private concern; that the others should have only delegated powers; and that this one should be designated by some general presumption of law, for example as being the eldest. The law never does this: nor does experience show it to be necessary that any theoretical inequality of power should exist between the partners, or that the partnership should have any other conditions than what they may themselves appoint by their articles of agreement. Yet it might seem that the exclusive power might be conceded with less danger to the rights and interests of the inferior, in the case of partnership than in that of marriage, since he is free to cancel the power by withdrawing from the connexion. The wife has no such power, and even if she had, it is almost always desirable that she should try all measures before resorting to it.

It is quite true that things which have to be decided every day, and cannot adjust themselves gradually, or wait for a compromise, ought to depend on one will; one person must have their sole control. But it does not follow that this should always be the same person. The natural arrangement is a division of powers between the two; each being absolute in the executive branch of their own department, and any change of system and principle requiring the consent of both. The division neither can nor should be pre-established by the law, since it must depend on individual capacities and suitabilities. If the two persons chose, they might pre-appoint it by the marriage contract, as pecuniary arrangements are now often pre-appointed. There would seldom be any difficulty in deciding such things by mutual consent, unless the marriage was one of those unhappy ones in which all other things, as well as this, become subjects of bickering and dispute. The division of rights would naturally follow the division of duties and functions; and that is already made by consent, or at all events not by law, but by general custom, modified and modifiable at the pleasure of the persons concerned.

The real practical decision of affairs, to whichever may be given the legal authority, will greatly depend, as it even now does, upon comparative qualifications. The mere fact that he is usually the eldest, will in most cases give the preponderance to the man; at least until they both attain a time of life at which the difference in their years is of no importance. There will naturally also be a more potential voice on the side, whichever it is, that brings the means of support. Inequality from this source does not depend on the law of marriage, but on the general conditions of human society, as now constituted. The influence of mental superiority, either general or special, and of superior decision of character, will necessarily tell for much. It always does so at present. And this fact shows how little foundation there is for the apprehension that the powers and responsibilities of partners in life (as of partners in business), cannot be satisfactorily apportioned by agreement between themselves. They always are so apportioned, except in cases in which the marriage institution is a failure. Things never come to an issue of downright power on one side, and obedience on the other, except where the connexion altogether has been a mistake, and it would be a blessing to both parties to be relieved from it. Some may say that the very thing by which an amicable settlement of differences becomes possible, is the power of legal compulsion known to be in reserve; as people submit to an arbitration because there is a court of law in the background, which they know that they can be forced to obey. But to make the cases parallel, we must suppose that the rule of the court of law was, not to try the cause, but to give judgment always for the same side, suppose the defendant. If so, the amenability to it would be a motive with the plaintiff to agree to almost any arbitration, but it would be just the reverse with the defendant. The despotic power which the law gives to the husband may be a reason to make the wife assent to any compromise by which power is practically shared between the two, but it cannot be the reason why the husband does. That there is always among decently conducted people a practical compromise, though one of them at least is under no physical or moral necessity of making it, shows that the natural motives which lead to a voluntary adjustment of the united life of two persons in a manner acceptable to both, do on the whole, except in unfavourable cases, prevail. The matter is certainly not improved by laying down as an ordinance of law, that the superstructure of free government shall be raised upon a legal basis of despotism on one side and subjection on the other, and that every concession which the despot makes may, at his mere pleasure, and without any warning, be recalled. Besides that no freedom is worth much when held on so precarious a tenure, its conditions are not likely to be the most equitable when the law throws so prodigious a weight into one scale; when the adjustment rests between two persons one of whom is declared to be entitled to everything, the other not only entitled to nothing except during the good pleasure of the first, but under the strongest moral and religious obligation not to rebel under any excess of oppression.

A pertinacious adversary, pushed to extremities, may say, that husbands indeed are willing to be reasonable, and to make fair concessions to their partners without being compelled to it, but that wives are not: that if allowed any rights of their own, they will acknowledge no rights at all in anyone else, and never will yield in anything, unless they can be compelled, by the man's mere authority, to yield in everything. This would have been said by many persons some generations ago, when satires on women were in vogue, and men thought it a clever thing to insult women for being what men made them. But it will be said by no·one now who is worth replying to. It is not the doctrine of the present day that women are less susceptible of good feeling, and consideration for those with whom they are united by the strongest ties, than men are. On the contrary, we are perpetually told that women are better than men, by those who are totally opposed to treating them as if they were as good; so that the saying has passed into a piece of tiresome cant, intended to put a complimentary face upon an injury, and resembling those celebrations of royal clemency which, according to Gulliver, the king of Lilliput always prefixed to his most sanguinary decrees. If women are better than men in anything, it surely is in individual self-sacrifice for those of their own family. But I lay little stress on this, so long as they are universally taught that they are born and created for self-sacrifice. I believe that equality of rights would abate the exaggerated self-abnegation which is the present artificial ideal of feminine character, and that a good woman would not be more self-sacrificing than the best man: but on the other hand, men would be much more unselfish and self-sacrificing than at present, because they would no longer be taught to worship their own will as such a grand thing that it is actually the law for another rational being. There is nothing which men so easily learn as this self-worship: all privileged persons, and all privileged classes, have had it. The more we descend in the scale of humanity, the intenser it is; and most of all in those who are not, and can never expect to be, raised above anyone except an unfortunate wife and children. The honourable exceptions are proportionally fewer than in the case of almost any other human infirmity. Philosophy and religion, instead of keeping it in check, are generally suborned to defend it; and nothing controls it but that practical feeling of the equality of human beings, which is the theory of Christianity, but which Christianity will never practically teach, while it sanctions institutions grounded on an arbitrary preference of one human being over another.

There are, no doubt, women, as there are men, whom equality of consideration will not satisfy; with whom there is no peace while any will or wish is regarded but their own. Such persons are a proper subject for the law of divorce. They are only fit to live alone, and no human beings ought to be compelled to associate their lives with them. But the legal subordination tends to make such characters among women more, rather than less, frequent. If the man exerts his whole power, the woman is of course crushed: but if she is treated with indulgence, and permitted to assume power, there is no rule to set limits to her encroachments. The law, not determining her rights, but theoretically allowing her none at all, practically declares that the measure of what she has a right to, is what she can contrive to get.

The equality of married persons before the law, is not only the sole mode in which that particular relation can be made consistent with justice to both sides, and conducive to the happiness of both, but it is the only means of rendering the daily life of mankind, in any high sense, a school of moral cultivation. Though the truth may not be felt or generally acknowledged for generations to come, the only school of genuine moral sentiment is society between equals. The moral education of mankind has hitherto emanated chiefly from the law of force, and is adapted almost solely to the relations which force creates. In the less advanced states of society, people hardly recognise any relation with their equals. To be an equal is to be an enemy. Society, from its highest place to its lowest, is one long chain, or rather ladder, where every individual is either above or below his nearest neighbour, and wherever he does not command he must obey. Existing moralities, accordingly, are mainly fitted to a relation of command and obedience. Yet command and obedience are but unfortunate necessities of human life: society in equality is its normal state. Already in modern life, and more and more as it progressively improves, command and obedience become exceptional facts in life, equal association its general rule. The morality of the first ages rested on the obligation to submit to power; that of the ages next following, on the right of the weak to the forbearance and protection of the strong. How much longer is one form of society and life to content itself with the morality made for another? We have had the morality of submission, and the morality of chivalry and generosity; the time is now come for the morality of justice. Whenever, in former ages, any approach has been made to society in equality, Justice has asserted its claims as the foundation of virtue. It was thus in the free republics of antiquity. But even in the best of these, the equals were limited to the free male citizens; slaves, women, and the unenfranchised residents were under the law of force. The joint influence of Roman civilisation and of Christianity obliterated these distinctions, and in theory (if only partially in practice) declared the claims of the human being, as such, to be paramount to those of sex, class, or social position. The barriers which had begun to be levelled were raised again by the northern conquests; and the whole of modern history consists of the slow process by which they have since been wearing away. We are entering into an order of things in which justice will again be the primary virtue; grounded as before on equal, but now also on sympathetic association; having its root no longer in the instinct of equals for self-protection, but in a cultivated sympathy between them; and no one being now left out, but an equal measure being extended to all. It is no novelty that mankind do not distinctly foresee their own changes, and that their sentiments are adapted to past, not to coming ages. To see the futurity of the species has always been the privilege of the intellectual élite, or of those who have learnt from them; to have the feelings of that futurity has been the distinction, and usually the martyrdom, of a still rarer élite. Institutions, books, education, society, all go on training human beings for the old, long after the new has come; much more when it is only coming. But the true virtue of human beings is fitness to live together as equals; claiming nothing for themselves but what they as freely concede to everyone else; regarding command of any kind as an exceptional necessity, and in all cases a temporary one; and preferring, whenever possible, the society of those with whom leading and following can be alternate and reciprocal. To these virtues, nothing in life as at present constituted gives cultivation by exercise. The family is a school of despotism, in which the virtues of despotism, but also its vices, are largely nourished. Citizenship, in free countries, is partly a school of society in equality; but citizenship fills only a small place in modern life, and does not come near the daily habits or inmost sentiments. The family, justly constituted, would be the real school of the virtues of freedom. It is sure to be a sufficient one of everything else. It will always be a school of obedience for the children, of command for the parents. What is needed is, that it should be a school of sympathy in equality, of living together in love, without power on one side or obedience on the other. This it ought to be between the parents. It would then be an exercise of those virtues which each requires to fit them for all other association, and a model to the children of the feelings and conduct which their temporary training by means of obedience is designed to render habitual, and therefore natural, to them. The moral training of mankind will never be adapted to the conditions of the life for which all other human progress is a preparation, until they practise in the family the same moral rule which is adapted to the normal constitution of human society. Any sentiment of freedom which can exist in a man whose nearest and dearest intimacies are with those of whom he is absolute master, is not the genuine or Christian love of freedom, but, what the love of freedom generally was in the ancients and in the middle ages—an intense feeling of the dignity and importance of his own personality; making him disdain a yoke for himself, of which he has no abhorrence whatever in the abstract, but which he is abundantly ready to impose on others for his own interest or glorification.

I readily admit (and it is the very foundation of my hopes) that numbers of married people even under the present law (in the higher classes of England probably a great majority), live in the spirit of a just law of equality. Laws never would be improved, if there were not numerous persons whose moral sentiments are better than the existing laws. Such persons ought to support the principles here advocated; of which the only object is to make all other married couples similar to what these are now. But persons even of considerable moral worth, unless they are also thinkers, are very ready to believe that laws or practices, the evils of which they have not personally experienced, do not produce any evils, but (if seeming to be generally approved of) probably do good, and that it is wrong to object to them. It would, however, be a great mistake in such married people to suppose, because the legal conditions of the tie which unites them do not occur to their thoughts once in a twelvemonth, and because they live and feel in all respects as if they were legally equals, that the same is the case with all other married couples, wherever the husband is not a notorious ruffian. To suppose this, would be to show equal ignorance of human nature and of fact. The less fit a man is for the possession of power—the less likely to be allowed to exercise it over any person with that person's voluntary consent—the more does he hug himself in the consciousness of the power the law gives him, exact its legal rights to the utmost point which custom (the custom of men like himself) will tolerate, and take pleasure in using the power, merely to enliven the agreeable sense of possessing it. What is more; in the most naturally brutal and morally uneducated part of the lower classes, the legal slavery of the woman, and something in the merely physical subjection to their will as an instrument, causes them to feel a sort of disrespect and contempt towards their own wife which they do not feel towards any other woman, or any other human being, with whom they come in contact; and which makes her seem to them an appropriate subject for any kind of indignity. Let an acute observer of the signs of feeling, who has the requisite opportunities, judge for himself whether this is not the case: and if he finds that it is, let him not wonder at any amount of disgust and indignation that can be felt against institutions which lead naturally to this depraved state of the human mind.

We shall be told, perhaps, that religion imposes the duty of obedience; as every established fact which is too bad to admit of any other defence, is always presented to us as an injunction of religion. The Church, it is very true, enjoins it in her formularies, but it would be difficult to derive any such injunction from Christianity. We are told that St. Paul said, "Wives, obey your husbands": but he also said, "Slaves, obey your masters." It was not St. Paul's business, nor was it consistent with his object, the propagation of Christianity, to incite anyone to rebellion against existing laws. The Apostle's acceptance of all social institutions as he found them, is no more to be construed as a disapproval of attempts to improve them at the proper time, than his declaration, "The powers that be are ordained of God," gives his sanction to military despotism, and to that alone, as the Christian form of political government, or commands passive obedience to it. To pretend that Christianity was intended to stereotype existing forms of government and society, and protect them against change, is to reduce it to the level of Islamism or of Brahminism. It is precisely because Christianity has not done this, that it has been the religion of the progressive portion of mankind, and Islamism, Brahminism, etc. have been those of the stationary portions; or rather (for there is no such thing as a really stationary society) of the declining portions. There have been abundance of people, in all ages of Christianity, who tried to make it something of the same kind; to convert us into a sort of Christian Mussulmans, with the Bible for a Koran, prohibiting all improvement: and great has been their power, and many have had to sacrifice their lives in resisting them. But they have been resisted, and the resistance has made us what we are, and will yet make us what we are to be.

After what has been said respecting the obligation of obedience, it is almost superfluous to say anything concerning the more special point included in the general one—a woman's right to her own property; for I need not hope that this treatise can make any impression upon those who need anything to convince them that a woman's inheritance or gains ought to be as much her own after marriage as before. The rule is simple: whatever would be the husband's or wife's if they were not married, should be under their exclusive control during marriage; which need not interfere with the power to tie up property by settlement, in order to preserve it for children. Some people are sentimentally shocked at the idea of a separate interest in money matters, as inconsistent with the ideal fusion of two lives into one. For my own part, I am one of the strongest supporters of community of goods, when resulting from an entire unity of feeling in the owners, which makes all things common between them. But I have no relish for a community of goods resting on the doctrine, that what is mine is yours, but what is yours is not mine; and I should prefer to decline entering into such a compact with anyone, though I were myself the person to profit by it.

This particular injustice and oppression to women, which is, to common apprehensions, more obvious than all the rest, admits of remedy without interfering with any other mischiefs: and there can be little doubt that it will be one of the earliest remedied. Already, in many of the new and several of the old States of the American Confederation, provisions have been inserted even in the written Constitutions, securing to women equality of rights in this respect: and thereby improving materially the position, in the marriage relation, of those women at least who have property, by leaving them one instrument of power which they have not signed away; and preventing also the scandalous abuse of the marriage institution, which is perpetrated when a man entraps a girl into marrying him without a settlement, for the sole purpose of getting possession of her money. When the support of the family depends, not on property, but on earnings, the common arrangement,

by which the man earns the income and the wife superintends
the domestic expenditure, seems to me in general the most
suitable division of labour between the two persons. If, in
addition to the physical suffering of bearing children, and the
whole responsibility of their care and education in early years,
the wife undertakes the careful and economical application of
the husband's earnings to the general comfort of the family;
she takes not only her fair share, but usually the larger share,
of the bodily and mental exertion required by their joint
existence. If she undertakes any additional portion, it seldom
relieves her from this, but only prevents her from performing
it properly. The care which she is herself disabled from taking
of the children and the household, nobody else takes; those of
the children who do not die, grow up as they best can, and the
management of the household is likely to be so bad, as even in
point of economy to be a great drawback from the value of the
wife's earnings. In an otherwise just state of things, it is not,
therefore, I think, a desirable custom, that the wife should
contribute by her labour to the income of the family. In an
unjust state of things, her doing so may be useful to her, by
making her of more value in the eyes of the man who is legally
her master; but, on the other hand, it enables him still farther
to abuse his power, by forcing her to work, and leaving the
support of the family to her exertions, while he spends most of
his time in drinking and idleness. The *power* of earning is
essential to the dignity of a woman, if she has not independent
property. But if marriage were an equal contract, not implying
the obligation of obedience; if the connexion were no longer
enforced to the oppression of those to whom it is purely a
mischief, but a separation, on just terms (I do not now speak
of a divorce), could be obtained by any woman who was morally
entitled to it; and if she would then find all honourable employments as freely open to her as to men; it would not be necessary
for her protection, that during marriage she should make this
particular use of her faculties. Like a man when he chooses
a profession, so, when a woman marries, it may in general be
understood that she makes choice of the management of a
household, and the bringing up of a family, as the first call upon
her exertions, during as many years of her life as may be
required for the purpose; and that she renounces, not all other
objects and occupations, but all which are not consistent with
the requirements of this. The actual exercise, in a habitual or
systematic manner, of outdoor occupations, or such as cannot

be carried on at home, would by this principle be practically interdicted to the greater number of married women. But the utmost latitude ought to exist for the adaptation of general rules to individual suitabilities; and there ought to be nothing to prevent faculties exceptionally adapted to any other pursuit, from obeying their vocation notwithstanding marriage: due provision being made for supplying otherwise any falling-short which might become inevitable, in her full performance of the ordinary functions of mistress of a family. These things, if once opinion were rightly directed on the subject, might with perfect safety be left to be regulated by opinion, without any interference of law.

CHAPTER III

On the other point which is involved in the just equality of women, their admissibility to all the functions and occupations hitherto retained as the monopoly of the stronger sex, I should anticipate no difficulty in convincing anyone who has gone with me on the subject of the equality of women in the family. I believe that their disabilities elsewhere are only clung to in order to maintain their subordination in domestic life; because the generality of the male sex cannot yet tolerate the idea of living with an equal. Were it not for that, I think that almost everyone, in the existing state of opinion in politics and political economy, would admit the injustice of excluding half the human race from the greater number of lucrative occupations, and from almost all high social functions; ordaining from their birth either that they are not, and cannot by any possibility become, fit for employments which are legally open to the stupidest and basest of the other sex, or else that however fit they may be, those employments shall be interdicted to them, in order to be preserved for the exclusive benefit of males. In the last two centuries, when (which was seldom the case) any reason beyond the mere existence of the fact was thought to be required to justify the disabilities of women, people seldom assigned as a reason their inferior mental capacity; which, in times when there was a real trial of personal faculties (from which all women were not excluded) in the struggles of public life, no one really believed in. The reason given in those days was not women's unfitness, but the interest of society, by which was meant the interest of men: just as the *raison d'état,* meaning the convenience of the government, and the support of existing authority, was deemed a sufficient explanation and excuse for the most flagitious crimes. In the present day, power holds a smoother language, and whomsoever it oppresses, always pretends to do so for their own good: accordingly, when anything is forbidden to women, it is thought necessary to say, and desirable to believe, that they are incapable of doing it, and that they depart from their real path of success and happiness when they aspire to it. But to make this reason plausible (I do not say valid), those by whom it is urged must be prepared to carry it to a much greater length than anyone ventures to do in the face of present experience. It is not sufficient to maintain that women on the average are less gifted then men on the average, with certain of the higher mental faculties, or that a smaller number of women than of men are fit for occupations and functions of the highest intellectual character. It is necessary to maintain that no women at all are fit for them, and that the most eminent women are inferior in mental faculties to the most mediocre of the men on whom those functions at present devolve. For if the performance of the function is decided either by competition, or by any mode of choice which secures regard to the public interest, there needs be no apprehension that any important employments will fall into the hands of women inferior to average men, or to the average of their male competitors. The only result would be that there would be fewer women than men in such employments; a result certain to happen in any case, if only from the preference always likely to be felt by the majority of women for the one vocation in which there is nobody to compete with them. Now, the most determined depreciator of women will not venture to deny, that when we add the experience of recent times to that of ages past, women, and not a few merely, but many women, have proved themselves capable of everything, perhaps without a single exception, which is done by men, and of doing it successfully and creditably. The utmost that can be said is, that there are many things which none of them have succeeded in doing as well as they have been done by some men—many in which they have not reached the very highest rank. But there are extremely few, dependent only on mental faculties, in which they have not attained the rank next to the highest. Is not this enough, and much more than enough, to make it a tyranny to them, and a detriment to society, that they should not be allowed to compete with men for the exercise of these functions? Is it not a mere truism to say, that such functions are often filled by men far less fit for them than numbers of women, and who would be beaten by women in any fair field of competition? What difference does it make that there may be men somewhere, fully employed about other things, who may be still better qualified for the things in question than these women? Does not this take place in all competitions? Is there so great a superfluity of men fit for high duties, that society can afford to reject the service of any competent person? Are we so certain of always finding a man made to our hands for any duty or function of social importance which falls vacant, that we lose nothing by putting a ban upon one half of mankind, and refusing beforehand to make their faculties available, however distinguished they may be? And even if we could do without them, would it be consistent with justice to refuse to them their fair share of honour and distinction, or to deny to them the equal moral right of all human beings to choose their occupation (short of injury to others) according to their own preferences, at their own risk? Nor is the injustice confined to them: it is shared by those who are in a position to benefit by their services. To ordain that any kind of persons shall not be physicians, or shall not be advocates, or shall not be Members of Parliament, is to injure not them only, but all who employ physicians or advocates, or elect Members of Parliament, and who are deprived of the stimulating effect of greater competition on the exertions of the competitors, as well as restricted to a narrower range of individual choice.

It will perhaps be sufficient if I confine myself, in the details of my argument, to functions of a public nature: since, if I am successful as to those, it probably will be readily granted that women should be admissible to all other occupations to which it is at all material whether they are admitted or not. And here let me begin by marking out one function, broadly distinguished from all others, their right to which is entirely independent of any question which can be raised concerning their faculties. I mean the suffrage, both parliamentary and municipal. The right to share in the choice of those who are to exercise a public trust, is altogether a distinct thing from that of competing for the trust itself. If no one could vote for a Member of Parliament who was not fit to be a candidate, the government would be a narrow oligarchy indeed. To have a voice in choosing those by whom one is to be governed, is a means of self-protection due to everyone, though he were to remain for ever excluded from the function of governing: and that women are considered fit to have such a choice, may be presumed from the fact, that the law already gives it to women in the most important of all cases to themselves: for the choice of the man who is to govern a woman to the end of life, is always supposed to be voluntarily made by herself. In the case of election to public trusts, it is the business of constitutional law to surround the right of suffrage with all needful securities and limitations; but whatever securities are sufficient in the case of the male sex, no others need be required in the case of women. Under whatever conditions, and within whatever limits, men are admitted to the suffrage, there is not a shadow of justification for not admitting women under the same. The majority of the women of any class are not likely to differ in political opinion from the majority of the men of the same class, unless the question be one in which the interests of women, as such, are in some way involved; and if they are so, women require the suffrage, as their guarantee of just and equal consideration. This ought to be obvious even to those who coincide in no other of the doctrines for which I contend. Even if every woman were a wife, and if every wife ought to be a slave, all the more would these slaves stand in need of legal protection: and we know what legal protection the slaves have, where the laws are made by their masters.

With regard to the fitness of women, not only to participate in elections, but themselves to hold offices or practise professions involving important public responsibilities; I have already observed that this consideration is not essential to the practical question in dispute: since any woman, who succeeds in an open profession, proves by that very fact that she is qualified for it. And in the case of public offices, if the political system of the country is such as to exclude unfit men, it will equally exclude unfit women: while if it is not, there is no additional evil in the fact that the unfit persons whom it admits may be either women or men. As long therefore as it is acknowledged that even a few women may be fit for these duties, the laws which shut the door on those exceptions cannot be justified by any opinion which can be held respecting the capacities of women in general. But, though this last consideration is not essential, it is far from being irrelevant. An unprejudiced view of it gives additional strength to the arguments against the disabilities of women, and reinforces them by high considerations of practical utility.

Let us first make entire abstraction of all psychological considerations tending to show, that any of the mental differences supposed to exist between women and men are but the natural effect of the differences in their education and circumstances, and indicate no radical difference, far less radical inferiority, of nature. Let us consider women only as they already are, or as they are known to have been; and the capacities which they have already practically shown. What they have done, that at least, if nothing else, it is proved that they can do. When we consider how sedulously they are all trained away from, instead of being trained towards, any of the occupations or objects reserved for men, it is evident that I am taking a very humble ground for them, when I rest their case on what they have actually achieved. For, in this case, negative evidence is worth little, while any positive evidence is conclusive. It cannot be inferred to be impossible that a woman should be a Homer, or an Aristotle, or a Michael Angelo, or a Beethoven, because no woman has yet actually produced works comparable to theirs in any of those lines of excellence. This negative fact at most leaves the question uncertain, and open to psychological discussion. But it is quite certain that a woman can be a Queen Elizabeth, or a Deborah, or a Joan of Arc, since this is not inference, but fact. Now it is a curious consideration, that the only things which the existing law excludes women from doing, are the things which they have proved that they are able to do. There is no law to prevent a woman from having written all the plays of Shakespeare, or composed all the operas of Mozart. But Queen Elizabeth or Queen Victoria, had they not inherited the throne, could not have been entrusted with the smallest of the political duties, of which the former showed herself equal to the greatest.

If anything conclusive could be inferred from experience, without psychological analysis, it would be that the things which women are not allowed to do are the very ones for which they are peculiarly qualified; since their vocation for government has made its way, and become conspicuous, through the very few opportunities which have been given; while in the lines of distinction which apparently were freely open to them, they have by no means so eminently distinguished themselves.

We know how small a number of reigning queens history presents, in comparison with that of kings. Of this smaller number a far larger proportion have shown talents for rule; though many of them have occupied the throne in difficult periods. It is remarkable, too, that they have, in a great number of instances, been distinguished by merits the most opposite to the imaginary and conventional character of women: they have been as much remarked for the firmness and vigour of their rule, as for its intelligence. When, to queens and empresses, we add regents, and viceroys of provinces, the list of women who have been eminent rulers of mankind swells to a great length.[1] This fact is so undeniable, that someone, long ago, tried to retort the argument, and turned the admitted truth into an additional insult, by saying that queens are better than kings, because under kings women govern, but under queens, men.

It may seem a waste of reasoning to argue against a bad joke; but such things do affect people's minds; and I have heard men quote this saying, with an air as if they thought that there was something in it. At any rate, it will serve as anything else for a starting-point in discussion. I say, then, that it is not true that under kings, women govern. Such cases are entirely exceptional: and weak kings have quite as often governed ill through the influence of male favourites, as of female. When a king is governed by a woman merely through his amatory propensities, good government is not probable, though even then there are exceptions. But French history counts two kings who have voluntarily given the direction of affairs during many years, the one to his mother, the other to his sister: one of them, Charles VIII, was a mere boy, but in doing so he followed the intentions of his father Louis XI, the ablest monarch of his age. The other, Saint Louis, was the best, and one of the most vigorous rulers, since the time of Charlemagne. Both these princesses ruled in a manner hardly equalled by any prince among their contemporaries. The Emperor Charles the Fifth, the most politic prince of his time, who had as great a number of able men in his service as a ruler ever had, and was one of the least likely of all sovereigns to sacrifice his interest to personal feelings, made two princesses of his family successively Governors of the Netherlands, and kept one or other of them in that post during his whole life (they were afterwards succeeded by a third). Both ruled very successfully,

[1] Especially is this true if we take into consideration Asia as well as Europe. If a Hindoo principality is strongly, vigilantly, and economically governed; if order is preserved without oppression; if cultivation is extending, and the people prosperous, in three cases out of four that principality is under a woman's rule. This fact, to me an entirely unexpected one, I have collected from a long official knowledge of Hindoo governments. There are many such instances: for though, by Hindoo institutions, a woman cannot reign, she is the legal regent of a kingdom during the minority of the heir; and minorities are frequent, the lives of the male rulers being so often prematurely terminated through the effect of inactivity and sensual excesses. When we consider that these princesses have never been seen in public, have never conversed with any man not of their own family except from behind a curtain, that they do not read, and if they did, there is no book in their languages which can give them the smallest instruction on political affairs; the example they afford of the natural capacity of women for government is very striking.

and one of them, Margaret of Austria, was one of the ablest politicians of the age. So much for one side of the question. Now as to the other. When it is said that under queens men govern, is the same meaning to be understood as when kings are said to be governed by women? Is it meant that queens choose as their instruments of government, the associates of their personal pleasures? The case is rare even with those who are as unscrupulous on the latter point as Catherine II: and it is not in these cases that the good government, alleged to arise from male influence, is to be found. If it be true, then, that the administration is in the hands of better men under a queen than under an average king, it must be that queens have a superior capacity for choosing them; and women must be better qualified than men both for the position of sovereign, and for that of chief minister; for the principal business of a Prime Minister is not to govern in person, but to find the fittest persons to conduct every department of public affairs. The more rapid insight into character, which is one of the admitted points of superiority in women over men, must certainly make them, with anything like parity of qualifications in other respects, more apt than men in that choice of instruments, which is nearly the most important business of everyone who has to do with governing mankind. Even the unprincipled Catherine de Medici could feel the value of a Chancellor de l'Hôpital. But it is also true that most great queens have been great by their own talents for government, and have been well served precisely for that reason. They retained the supreme direction of affairs in their own hands: and if they listened to good advisers, they gave by that fact the strongest proof that their judgment fitted them for dealing with the great questions of government.

Is it reasonable to think that those who are fit for the greater functions of politics, are incapable of qualifying themselves for the less? Is there any reason in the nature of things, that the wives and sisters of princes should, whenever called on, be found as competent as the princes themselves to *their* business, but that the wives and sisters of statesmen, and administrators, and directors of companies, and managers of public institutions, should be unable to do what is done by their brothers and husbands? The real reason is plain enough; it is that princesses, being more raised above the generality of men by their rank than placed below them by their sex, have never been taught that it was improper for them to concern themselves with politics; but have been allowed to feel the liberal interest natural to any cultivated human being, in the great transactions which took place around them, and in which they might be called on to take a part. The ladies of reigning families are the only women who are allowed the same range of interests and freedom of development as men; and it is precisely in their case that there is not found to be any inferiority. Exactly where and in proportion as women's capacities for government have been tried, in that proportion have they been found adequate.

This fact is in accordance with the best general conclusions which the world's imperfect experience seems as yet to suggest, concerning the peculiar tendencies and aptitudes characteristic of women, as women have hitherto been. I do not say, as they will continue to be; for, as I have already said more than once, I consider it presumption in anyone to pretend to decide what women are or are not, can or cannot be, by natural constitution. They have always hitherto been kept, as far as regards spontaneous development, in so unnatural a state, that their nature cannot but have been greatly distorted and disguised; and no one can safely pronounce that if women's nature were left to choose its direction as freely as men's, and if no artificial bent were attempted to be given to it except that required by the conditions of human society, and given to both sexes alike, there would be any material difference, or perhaps any difference at all, in the character and capacities which would unfold themselves. I shall presently show, that even the least contestable of the differences which now exist, are such as may very well have been produced merely by circumstances, without any difference of natural capacity. But, looking at women as they are known in experience, it may be said of them, with more truth than belongs to most other generalisations on the subject, that the general bent of their talents is towards the practical. This statement is conformable to all the public history of women, in the present and the past. It is no less borne out by common and daily experience. Let us consider the special nature of the mental capacities most characteristic of a woman of talent. They are all of a kind which fits them for practice, and makes them tend towards it. What is meant by a woman's capacity of intuitive perception? It means, a rapid and correct insight into present fact. It has nothing to do with general principles. Nobody ever perceived a scientific law of nature by intuition, nor arrived at a general rule of duty or prudence by it. These are results of slow and careful collection and comparison of experience; and neither the men nor the women of intuition usually shine in this department, unless, indeed, the experience necessary is such as they can acquire by themselves. For what is called their intuitive sagacity makes them peculiarly apt in gathering such general truths as can be collected from their individual means of observation. When, consequently, they chance to be as well provided as men are with the results of other people's experience, by reading and education (I use the word chance advisedly, for, in respect to the knowledge that tends to fit them for the greater concerns of life, the only educated women are the self-educated) they are better furnished than men in general with the essential requisites of skilful and successful practice. Men who have been much taught, are apt to be deficient in the sense of present fact; they do not see, in the facts which they are called upon to deal with, what is really there, but what they have been taught to expect. This is seldom the case with women of any ability. Their capacity of "intuition" preserves them from it. With equality of experience and of general faculties, a woman usually sees much more than a man of what is immediately before her. Now this sensibility to the present, is the main quality on which the capacity for practice, as distinguished from theory, depends. To discover general principles, belongs to the speculative faculty: to discern and discriminate the particular cases in which they are and are not applicable, constitutes practical talent: and for this, women as they now are have a peculiar aptitude. I admit that there can be no good practice without principles, and that the predominant place which quickness of observation holds among a woman's faculties, makes her particularly apt to build overhasty generalisations upon her own observation; though at the same time no less ready in rectifying those generalisations, as her observation takes a wider range. But the corrective to this defect, is access to the experience of the human race; general knowledge—exactly the thing which education can best supply. A woman's mistakes are specifically those of a clever self-educated man, who often sees what men trained in routine do not see, but falls into errors for want of knowing things which have long been known. Of course he has acquired much of the pre-existing knowledge, or he could not have got on at all; but what he knows of it he has picked up in fragments and at random, as women do.

But this gravitation of women's minds to the present, to the real, to actual fact, while in its exclusiveness it is a source of errors, is also a most useful counteractive of the contrary error. The principal and most characteristic aberration of speculative minds as such, consists precisely in the deficiency of this lively perception and ever-present sense of objective fact. For want of this, they often not only overlook the contradiction which outward facts oppose to their theories, but lose sight of the legitimate purpose of speculation altogether, and let their speculative faculties go astray into regions not peopled with real beings, animate or inanimate, even idealised, but with personified shadows created by the illusions of metaphysics or by the mere entanglement of words, and think these shadows the proper objects of the highest, the most transcendant, philosophy. Hardly anything can be of greater value to a man of theory and speculation who employs himself not in collecting materials of knowledge by observation, but in working them up by processes of thought into comprehensive truths of science and laws of conduct, than to carry on his speculations in the companionship, and under the criticism, of a really superior woman. There is nothing comparable to it for keeping his thoughts within the limits of real things, and the actual facts of nature. A woman seldom runs wild after an abstraction. The habitual direction of her mind to dealing with things as individuals rather than in groups, and (what is closely connected with it) her more lively interest in the present feelings of persons, which makes her consider first of all, in anything which claims to be applied to practice, in what manner persons will be affected by it— these two things make her extremely unlikely to put faith in any speculation which loses sight of individuals, and deals with things as if they existed for the benefit of some imaginary entity, some mere creation of the mind, not resolvable into the feelings of living beings. Women's thoughts are thus as useful in giving reality to those of thinking men, as men's thoughts in giving width and largeness to those of women. In depth, as distinguished from breadth, I greatly doubt if even now, women, compared with men, are at any disadvantage.

If the existing mental characteristics of women are thus valuable even in aid of speculation, they are still more important, when speculation has done its work, for carrying out the results of speculation into practice. For the reasons already given, women are comparatively unlikely to fall into the common error of men, that of sticking to their rules in a case whose specialities either take it out of the class to which the rules are applicable, or require a special adaptation of them. Let us now consider another of the admitted superiorities of clever women, greater quickness of apprehension. Is not this pre-eminently a quality which fits a person for practice? In action, everything continually depends upon deciding promptly. In speculation, nothing does. A mere thinker can wait, can take time to consider, can collect additional evidence; he is not obliged to complete his philosophy at once, lest the opportunity should go by. The power of drawing the best conclusion possible from insufficient data is not indeed useless in philosophy; the construction of a provisional hypothesis consistent with all known facts is often the needful basis for further inquiry. But this faculty is rather serviceable in philosophy, than the main qualification for it: and, for the auxiliary as well as for the main operation, the philosopher can allow himself any time he pleases. He is in no need of the capacity of doing rapidly what he does; what he rather needs is patience, to work on slowly until imperfect lights have become perfect, and a conjecture has ripened into a theorem. For those, on the contrary, whose business is with the fugitive and perishable—with individual facts, not kinds of facts—rapidity of thought is a qualification next only in importance to the power of thought itself. He who has not his faculties under. immediate command, in the contingencies of action, might as well not have them at all. He may be fit to criticise, but he is not fit to act. Now it is in this that women, and the men who are most like women, confessedly excel. The other sort of man, however pre-eminent may be his faculties, arrives slowly at complete command of them: rapidity of judgment and promptitude of judicious action, even in the things he knows best, are the gradual and late result of strenuous effort grown into habit.

It will be said, perhaps, that the greater nervous susceptibility of women is a disqualification for practice, in anything but domestic life, by rendering them mobile, changeable, too vehemently under the influence of the moment, incapable of dogged perseverance, unequal and uncertain in the power of using their faculties. I think that these phrases sum up the greater part of the objections commonly made to the fitness of women for the higher class of serious business. Much of all this is the mere overflow of nervous energy run to waste, and would cease when the energy was directed to a definite end. Much is also the result of conscious or unconscious cultivation; as we see by the almost total disappearance of "hysterics" and fainting-fits, since they have gone out of fashion. Moreover, when people are brought up, like many women of the higher classes (though less so in our own country than in any other), a kind of hot-house plants, shielded from the wholesome vicissitudes of air and temperature, and untrained in any of the occupations and exercises which give stimulus and development to the circulatory and muscular system, while their nervous system, especially in its emotional department, is kept in unnaturally active play; it is no wonder if those of them who do not die of consumption, grow up with constitutions liable to derangement from slight causes, both internal and external, and without stamina to support any task, physical or mental, requiring continuity of effort. But women brought up to work for their livelihood show none of these morbid characteristics, unless indeed they are chained to an excess of sedentary work in confined and unhealthy rooms. Women who in their early years have shared in the healthful physical education and bodily freedom of their brothers, and who obtain a sufficiency of pure air and exercise in after-life, very rarely have any excessive susceptibility of nerves which can disqualify them for active pursuits. There is indeed a certain proportion of persons, in both sexes, in whom an unusual degree of nervous sensibility is constitutional, and of so marked a character as to be the feature of their organisation which exercises the greatest influence over the whole character of the vital phenomena. This constitution, like other physical conformations, is hereditary, and is transmitted to sons as well as daughters; but it is possible, and probable, that the nervous temperament (as it is called) is inherited by a greater number of women than of men. We will assume this as a fact: and let me then ask, are men of nervous temperament found to be unfit for the duties and pursuits usually followed by men? If not, why should women of the same temperament be unfit for them? The peculiarities of the temperament are, no doubt, within certain limits, an obstacle to success in some employments, though an aid to it in others. But when the occupation is suitable to the temperament, and sometimes even when it is unsuitable, the most brilliant examples of success are continually given by the men of high nervous sensibility. They are distinguished in their practical manifestations chiefly by this, that being susceptible of a higher degree of excitement than those of another physical constitution, their powers when excited differ more than in the case of other people, from those shown in their ordinary state: they are raised, as it were, above themselves, and do things

K 8&5

with ease which they are wholly incapable of at other times. But this lofty excitement is not, except in weak bodily constitutions, a mere flash, which passes away immediately, leaving no permanent traces, and incompatible with persistent and steady pursuit of an object. It is the character of the nervous temperament to be capable of *sustained* excitement, holding out through long-continued efforts. It is what is meant by *spirit*. It is what makes the high-bred racehorse run without slackening speed till he drops down dead. It is what has enabled so many delicate women to maintain the most sublime constancy not only at the stake, but through a long preliminary succession of mental and bodily tortures. It is evident that people of this temperament are particularly apt for what may be called the executive department of the leadership of mankind. They are the material of great orators, great preachers, impressive diffusers of moral influences. Their constitution might be deemed less favourable to the qualities required from a statesman in the cabinet, or from a judge. It would be so, if the consequence necessarily followed that because people are excitable they must always be in a state of excitement. But this is wholly a question of training. Strong feeling is the instrument and element of strong self-control: but it requires to be cultivated in that direction. When it is, it forms not the heroes of impulse only, but those also of self-conquest. History and experience prove that the most passionate characters are the most fanatically rigid in their feelings of duty, when their passion has been trained to act in that direction. The judge who gives a just decision in a case where his feelings are intensely interested on the other side, derives from that same strength of feeling the determined sense of the obligation of justice, which enables him to achieve this victory over himself. The capability of that lofty enthusiasm which takes the human being out of his every-day character, reacts upon the daily character itself. His aspirations and powers when he is in this exceptional state, become the type with which he compares, and by which he estimates, his sentiments and proceedings at other times: and his habitual purposes assume a character moulded by and assimilated to the moments of lofty excitement, although those, from the physical nature of a human being, can only be transient. Experience of races, as well as of individuals, does not show those of excitable temperament to be less fit, on the average, either for speculation or practice, than the more unexcitable. The French, and the Italians, are undoubtedly by nature more nervously excitable than the Teutonic races, and, compared at least with the English, they have a much greater habitual and daily emotional life: but have they been less great in science, in public business, in legal and judicial eminence, or in war? There is abundant evidence that the Greeks were of old, as their descendants and successors still are, one of the most excitable of the races of mankind. It is superfluous to ask, what among the achievements of men they did not excel in. The Romans, probably, as an equally southern people, had the same original temperament: but the stern character of their national discipline, like that of the Spartans, made them an example of the opposite type of national character; the greater strength of their natural feelings being chiefly apparent in the intensity which the same original temperament made it possible to give to the artificial. If these cases exemplify what a naturally excitable people may be made, the Irish Celts afford one of the aptest examples of what they are when left to themselves; (if those can be said to be left to themselves who have been for centuries under the indirect influence of bad government, and the direct training of a Catholic hierarchy and of a sincere belief in the Catholic religion). The Irish character must be considered, therefore, as an unfavourable case: yet, whenever the circumstances of the individual have been at all favourable, what people have shown greater capacity for the most varied and multifarious individual eminence? Like the French compared with the English, the Irish with the Swiss, the Greeks or Italians compared with the German races, so women compared with men may be found, on the average, to do the same things with some variety in the particular kind of excellence. But, that they would do them fully as well on the whole, if their education and cultivation were adapted to correcting instead of aggravating the infirmities incident to their temperament, I see not the smallest reason to doubt.

Supposing it, however, to be true that women's minds are by nature more mobile than those of men, less capable of persisting long in the same continuous effort, more fitted for dividing their faculties among many things than for travelling in any one path to the highest point which can be reached by it: this may be true of women as they now are (though not without great and numerous exceptions), and may account for their having remained behind the highest order of men in precisely the things in which this absorption of the whole mind in one set of ideas and occupations may seem to be most requisite.

Still, this difference is one which can only affect the kind of excellence, not the excellence itself, or its practical worth: and it remains to be shown whether this exclusive working of a part of the mind, this absorption of the whole thinking faculty in a single subject, and concentration of it on a single work, is the normal and healthful condition of the human faculties, even for speculative uses. I believe that what is gained in special development by this concentration, is lost in the capacity of the mind for the other purposes of life; and even in abstract thought, it is my decided opinion that the mind does more by frequently returning to a difficult problem, than by sticking to it without interruption. For the purposes, at all events, of practice, from its highest to its humblest departments, the capacity of passing promptly from one subject of consideration to another, without letting the active spring of the intellect run down between the two, is a power far more valuable; and this power women pre-eminently possess, by virtue of the very mobility of which they are accused. They perhaps have it from nature, but they certainly have it by training and education; for nearly the whole of the occupations of women consist in the management of small but multitudinous details, on each of which the mind cannot dwell even for a minute, but must pass on to other things, and if anything requires longer thought, must steal time at odd moments for thinking of it. The capacity indeed which women show for doing their thinking in circumstances and at times which almost any man would make an excuse to himself for not attempting it, has often been noticed: and a woman's mind, though it may be occupied only with small things, can hardly ever permit itself to be vacant, as a man's so often is when not engaged in what he chooses to consider the business of his life. The business of a woman's ordinary life is things in general, and can as little cease to go on as the world to go round.

But (it is said) there is anatomical evidence of the superior mental capacity of men compared with women: they have a larger brain. I reply, that in the first place the fact itself is doubtful. It is by no means established that the brain of a woman is smaller than that of a man. If it is inferred merely because a woman's bodily frame generally is of less dimensions than a man's, this criterion would lead to strange consequences. A tall and large-boned man must on this showing be wonderfully superior in intelligence to a small man, and an elephant or a whale must prodigiously excel mankind. The size of the brain in human beings, anatomists say, varies much less than the size of the body, or even of the head, and the one cannot be at all inferred from the other. It is certain that some women have as large a brain as any man. It is within my knowledge that a man who had weighed many human brains, said that the heaviest he knew of, heavier even than Cuvier's (the heaviest previously recorded), was that of a woman. Next, I must observe that the precise relation which exists between the brain and the intellectual powers is not yet well understood, but is a subject of great dispute. That there is a very close relation we cannot doubt. The brain is certainly the material organ of thought and feeling: and (making abstraction of the great unsettled controversy respecting the appropriation of different parts of the brain to different mental faculties) I admit that it would be an anomaly, and an exception to all we know of the general laws of life and organisation, if the size of the organ were wholly indifferent to the function; if no accession of power were derived from the great magnitude of the instrument. But the exception and the anomaly would be fully as great if the organ exercised influence by its magnitude *only*. In all the more delicate operations of nature—of which those of the animated creation are the most delicate, and those of the nervous system by far the most delicate of these—differences in the effect depend as much on differences of quality in the physical agents, as on their quantity: and if the quality of an instrument is to be tested by the nicety and delicacy of the work it can do, the indications point to a greater average fineness of quality in the brain and nervous system of women than of men. Dismissing abstract difference of quality, a thing difficult to verify, the efficiency of an organ is known to depend not solely on its size but on its activity: and of this we have an approximate measure in the energy with which the blood circulates through it, both the stimulus and the reparative force being mainly dependent on the circulation. It would not be surprising—it is indeed an hypothesis which accords well with the differences actually observed between the mental operations of the two sexes—if men on the average should have the advantage in the size of the brain, and women in activity of cerebral circulation. The results which conjecture, founded on analogy, would lead us to expect from this difference of organisation, would correspond to some of those which we most commonly see. In the first place, the mental operations of men might be expected to be slower. They would neither be so prompt as women in thinking, nor so quick to feel. Large bodies take more time to get into full action. On the other hand, when once got thoroughly into play, men's brain would bear more work. It would be more persistent in the line first taken; it would have more difficulty in changing from one mode of action to another, but, in the one thing it was doing, it could go on longer without loss of power or sense of fatigue. And do we not find that the things in which men most excel women are those which require most plodding and long hammering at a single thought, while women do best what must be done rapidly? A woman's brain is sooner fatigued, sooner exhausted; but given the degree of exhaustion, we should expect to find that it would recover itself sooner. I repeat that this speculation is entirely hypothetical; it pretends to no more than to suggest a line of inquiry. I have before repudiated the notion of its being yet certainly known that there is any natural difference at all in the average strength or direction of the mental capacities of the two sexes, much less what that difference is. Nor is it possible that this should be known, so long as the psychological laws of the formation of character have been so little studied, even in a general way, and in the particular case never scientifically applied at all; so long as the most obvious external causes of difference of character are habitually disregarded—left unnoticed by the observer, and looked down upon with a kind of supercilious contempt by the prevalent schools both of natural history and of mental philosophy: who, whether they look for the source of what mainly distinguishes human beings from one another, in the world of matter or in that of spirit, agree in running down those who prefer to explain these differences by the different relations of human beings to society and life.

To so ridiculous an extent are the notions formed of the nature of women, mere empirical generalisations, framed, without philosophy or analysis, upon the first instances which present themselves, that the popular idea of it is different in different countries, according as the opinions and social circumstances of the country have given to the women living in it any speciality of development or non-development. An Oriental thinks that women are by nature peculiarly voluptuous; see the violent abuse of them on this ground in Hindoo writings. An Englishman usually thinks that they are by nature cold. The sayings about women's fickleness are mostly of French origin; from the famous distich of Francis the First, upward and downward. In England it is a common remark, how much more constant women are than men. Inconstancy has been longer reckoned discreditable to a woman, in England than in France; and Englishwomen are besides, in their inmost nature, much more subdued to opinion. It may be remarked by the way, that Englishmen are in peculiarly unfavourable circumstances for attempting to judge what is or is not natural, not merely to women, but to men, or to human beings altogether, at least if they have only English experience to go upon: because there is no place where human nature shows so little of its original lineaments. Both in a good and a bad sense, the English are farther from a state of nature than any other modern people. They are, more than any other people, a product of civilisation and discipline. England is the country in which social discipline has most succeeded, not so much in conquering, as in suppressing, whatever is liable to conflict with it. The English, more than any other people, not only act but feel according to rule. In other countries, the taught opinion, or the requirement of society, may be the stronger power, but the promptings of the individual nature are always visible under it, and often resisting it: rule may be stronger than nature, but nature is still there. In England, rule has to a great degree substituted itself for nature. The greater part of life is carried on, not by following inclination under the control of rule, but by having no inclination but that of following a rule. Now this has its good side doubtless, though it has also a wretchedly bad one; but it must render an Englishman peculiarly ill-qualified to pass a judgmen; on the original tendencies of human nature from his own experience. The errors to which observers elsewhere are liable on the subject, are of a different character. An Englishman is ignorant respecting human nature, a Frenchman is prejudiced. An Englishman's errors are negative, a Frenchman's positive. An Englishman fancies that things do not exist, because he never sees them; a Frenchman thinks they must always and necessarily exist, because he does see them. An Englishman does not know nature, because he has had no opportunity of observing it; a Frenchman generally knows a great deal of it, but often mistakes it, because he has only seen it sophisticated and distorted. For the artificial state superinduced by society disguises the natural tendencies of the thing which is the subject of observation, in two different ways: by extinguishing the nature, or by transforming it. In the one case there is but a starved residuum of nature remaining to be studied; in the other case there is much, but it may have expanded in any direction rather than that in which it would spontaneously grow.

I have said that it cannot now be known how much of the existing mental differences between men and women is natural, and how much artificial; whether there are any natural differences at all; or, supposing all artificial causes of difference to be withdrawn, what natural character would be revealed. I am not about to attempt what I have pronounced impossible: but doubt does not forbid conjecture, and where certainty is unattainable, there may yet be the means of arriving at some degree of probability. The first point, the origin of the differences actually observed, is the one most accessible to speculation; and I shall attempt to approach it, by the only path by which it can be reached; by tracing the mental consequences of external influences. We cannot isolate a human being from the circumstances of his condition, so as to ascertain experimentally what he would have been by nature; but we can consider what he is, and what his circumstances have been, and whether the one would have been capable of producing the other.

Let us take, then, the only marked case which observation affords, of apparent inferiority of women to men, if we except the merely physical one of bodily strength. No production in philosophy, science, or art, entitled to the first rank, has been the work of a woman. Is there any mode of accounting for this, without supposing that women are naturally incapable of producing them?

In the first place, we may fairly question whether experience has afforded sufficient grounds for an induction. It is scarcely three generations since women, saving very rare exceptions, have begun to try their capacity in philosophy, science, or art. It is only in the present generation that their attempts have been at all numerous; and they are even now extremely few, everywhere but in England and France. It is a relevant question, whether a mind possessing the requisites of first-rate eminence in speculation or creative art could have been expected, on the mere calculation of chances, to turn up during that lapse of time, among the women whose tastes and personal position admitted of their devoting themselves to these pursuits. In all things which there has yet been time for—in all but the very highest grades in the scale of excellence, especially in the department in which they have been longest engaged, literature (both prose and poetry)—women have done quite as much, have obtained fully as high prizes and as many of them, as could be expected from the length of time and the number of competitors. If we go back to the earlier period when very few women made the attempt, yet some of those few made it with distinguished success. The Greeks always accounted Sappho among their great poets; and we may well suppose that Myrtis, said to have been the teacher of Pindar, and Corinna, who five times bore away from him the prize of poetry, must at least have had sufficient merit to admit of being compared with that great name. Aspasia did not leave any philosophical writings; but it is an admitted fact that Socrates resorted to her for instruction, and avowed himself to have obtained it.

If we consider the works of women in modern times, and contrast them with those of men, either in the literary or the artistic department, such inferiority as may be observed resolves itself essentially into one thing: but that is a most material one; deficiency of originality. Not total deficiency; for every production of mind which is of any substantive value, has an originality of its own—is a conception of the mind itself, not a copy of something else. Thoughts original, in the sense of being unborrowed—of being derived from the thinker's own observations or intellectual processes—are abundant in the writings of women. But they have not yet produced any of those great and luminous new ideas which form an era in thought, nor those fundamentally new conceptions in art, which open a vista of possible effects not before thought of, and found a new school. Their compositions are mostly grounded on the existing fund of thought, and their creations do not deviate widely from existing types. This is the sort of inferiority which their works manifest: for in point of execution, in the detailed application of thought, and the perfection of style, there is no inferiority. Our best novelists in point of composition, and of the management of detail, have mostly been women; and there is not in all modern literature a more eloquent vehicle of thought than the style of Madame de Staël, nor, as a specimen of purely artistic excellence, anything superior to the prose of Madame Sand, whose style acts upon the nervous system like a symphony of Haydn or Mozart. High originality of conception is, as I have said, what is chiefly wanting. And now to examine if there is any manner in which this deficiency can be accounted for.

Let us remember, then, so far as regards mere thought, that during all that period in the world's existence, and in the progress of cultivation, in which great and fruitful new truths could be arrived at by mere force of genius, with little previous study and accumulation of knowledge—during all that time women did not concern themselves with speculation at all. From the days of Hypatia to those of the Reformation, the illustrious Heloisa is almost the only woman to whom any such achievement might have been possible; and we know not how great a capacity of speculation in her may have been lost to mankind by the misfortunes of her life. Never since any considerable number of women have began to cultivate serious thought, has originality been possible on easy terms. Nearly all the thoughts which can be reached by mere strength of original faculties, have long since been arrived at; and originality, in any high sense of the word, is now scarcely ever attained but by minds which have undergone elaborate discipline, and are deeply versed in the results of previous thinking. It is Mr. Maurice, I think, who has remarked on the present age, that its most original thinkers are those who have known most thoroughly what had been thought by their predecessors: and this will always henceforth be the case. Every fresh stone in the edifice has now to be placed on the top of so many others, that a long process of climbing, and of carrying up materials, has to be gone through by whoever aspires to take a share in the present stage of the work. How many women are there who have gone through any such process? Mrs. Somerville, alone perhaps of women, knows as much of mathematics as is now needful for making any considerable mathematical discovery: is it any proof of inferiority in women, that she has not happened to be one of the two or three persons who in her lifetime have associated their names with some striking advancement of the science? Two women, since political economy has been made a science, have known enough of it to write usefully on the subject: of how many of the innumerable men who have written on it during the same time, is it possible with truth to say more? If no woman has hitherto been a great historian, what woman has had the necessary erudition? If no woman is a great philologist, what woman has studied Sanscrit and Slavonic, the Gothic of Ulphila and the Persic of the Zendavesta? Even in practical matters we all know what is the value of the originality of untaught geniuses. It means, inventing over again in its rudimentary form something already invented and improved upon by many successive inventors. When women have had the preparation which all men now require to be eminently original, it will be time enough to begin judging by experience of their capacity for originality.

It no doubt often happens that a person, who has not widely and accurately studied the thoughts of others on a subject, has by natural sagacity a happy intuition, which he can suggest, but cannot prove, which yet when matured may be an important addition to knowledge: but even then, no justice can be done to it until some other person, who does possess the previous acquirements, takes it in hand, tests it, gives it a scientific or practical form, and fits it into its place among the existing truths of philosophy or science. Is it supposed that such felicitous thoughts do not occur to women? They occur by hundreds to every woman of intellect. But they are mostly lost, for want of a husband or friend who has the other knowledge which can enable him to estimate them properly and bring them before the world: and even when they are brought before it, they generally appear as his ideas, not their real author's. Who can tell how many of the most original thoughts put forth by male writers, belong to a woman by suggestion, to themselves only by verifying and working out? If I may judge by my own case, a very large proportion indeed.

If we turn from pure speculation to literature in the narrow sense of the term, and the fine arts, there is a very obvious reason why women's literature is, in its general conception and in its main features, an imitation of men's. Why is the Roman literature, as critics proclaim to satiety, not original, but an imitation of the Greek? Simply because the Greeks came first. If women lived in a different country from men, and had never read any of their writings, they would have had a literature of their own. As it is, they have not created one, because they found a highly advanced literature already created. If there had been no suspension of the knowledge of antiquity, or if the Renaissance had occurred before the Gothic cathedrals were built, they never would have been built. We see that, in France and Italy, imitation of the ancient literature stopped the original development even after it had commenced. All women who write are pupils of the great male writers. A painter's early pictures, even if he be a Raffaello, are undistinguishable in style from those of his master. Even a Mozart does not display his powerful originality in his earliest pieces. What years are to a gifted individual, generations are to a mass. If women's literature is destined to have a different collective character from that of men, depending on any difference of natural tendencies, much longer time is necessary than has yet elapsed, before it can emancipate itself from the influence of accepted models, and guide itself by its own impulses. But if, as I believe, there will not prove to be any natural tendencies common to women, and distinguishing their genius from that of men, yet every individual writer among them has her individual tendencies, which at present are still subdued by the influence of precedent and example: and it will require generations more, before their individuality is sufficiently developed to make head against that influence.

It is in the fine arts, properly so called, that the prima facie evidence of inferior original powers in women at first sight appears the strongest: since opinion (it may be said) does not exclude them from these, but rather encourages them, and their education, instead of passing over this department, is in the affluent classes mainly composed of it. Yet in this line of exertion they have fallen still more short than in many others, of the highest eminence attained by men. This shortcoming, however, needs no other explanation than the familiar fact, more universally true in the fine arts than in anything else; the vast superiority of professional persons over amateurs. Women in the educated classes are almost universally taught more or less of some branch or other of the fine arts, but not that they may gain their living or their social consequence by it. Women artists are all amateurs. The exceptions are only of the kind which confirm the general truth. Women are taught music, but not for the purpose of composing, only of executing it: and accordingly it is only as composers, that men, in music, are superior to women. The only one of the fine arts which women do follow, to any extent, as a profession, and an occupation for life, is the histrionic; and in that they are confessedly equal, if not superior, to men. To make the comparison fair, it should be made between the productions of women in any branch of art, and those of men not following it as a profession. In musical composition, for example, women surely have produced fully as good things as have ever been produced by male amateurs. There are now a few women, a very few, who practise painting as a profession, and these are already beginning to show quite as much talent as could be expected. Even male painters (*pace* Mr. Ruskin) have not made any very remarkable figure these last centuries, and it will be long before they do so. The reason why the old painters were so greatly superior to the modern, is that a greatly superior class of men applied themselves to the art. In the fourteenth and fifteenth centuries the Italian painters were the most accomplished men of their age. The greatest of them were men of encyclopædical acquirements and powers, like the great men of Greece. But in their times fine art was, to men's feelings and conceptions, among the grandest things in which a human being could excel; and by it men were made, what only political or military distinction now makes them, the companions of sovereigns, and the equals of the highest nobility. In the present age, men of anything like similar calibre find something more important to do, for their own fame and the uses of the modern world, than painting: and it is only now and then that a Reynolds or a Turner (of whose relative rank among eminent men I do not pretend to an opinion) applies himself to that art. Music belongs to a different order of things: it does not require the same general powers of mind, but seems more dependent on a natural gift: and it may be thought surprising that no one of the great musical composers has been a woman. But even this natural gift, to be made available for great creations, requires study, and professional devotion to the pursuit. The only countries which have produced first-rate composers, even of the male sex, are Germany and Italy—countries in which, both in point of special and of general cultivation, women have remained far behind France and England, being generally (it may be said without exaggeration) very little educated, and having scarcely cultivated at all any of the higher faculties of mind. And in those countries the men who are acquainted with the principles of musical composition must be counted by hundreds, or more probably by thousands, the women barely by scores: so that here again, on the doctrine of averages, we cannot reasonably expect to see more than one eminent woman to fifty eminent men; and the last three centuries have not produced fifty eminent male composers either in Germany or in Italy.

There are other reasons, besides those which we have now given, that help to explain why women remain behind men, even in the pursuits which are open to both. For one thing, very few women have time for them. This may seem a paradox; it is an undoubted social fact. The time and thoughts of every woman have to satisfy great previous demands on them for things practical. There is, first, the superintendence of the family and the domestic expenditure, which occupies at least one woman in every family, generally the one of mature years and acquired experience; unless the family is so rich as to admit of delegating that task to hired agency, and submitting to all the waste and malversation inseparable from that mode of conducting it. The superintendence of a household, even when not in other respects laborious, is extremely onerous to the thoughts; it requires incessant vigilance, an eye which no detail escapes, and presents questions for consideration and solution, foreseen and unforeseen, at every hour of the day, from which the person responsible for them can hardly ever shake herself free. If a woman is of a rank and circumstances which relieve her in a measure from these cares, she has still devolving on her the management for the whole family of its intercourse with others—of what is called society, and the less the call made on her by the former duty, the greater is always the development of the latter: the dinner parties, concerts, evening parties, morning visits, letter-writing, and all that goes with them. All this is over and above the engrossing duty which society imposes exclusively on women, of making themselves charming. A clever woman of the higher ranks finds nearly a sufficient employment of her talents in cultivating the graces of manner and the arts of conversation. To look only at the outward side of the subject: the great and continual exercise of thought which all women who attach any value to dressing well (I do not mean expensively, but with taste, and perception of natural and of artificial *convenance*) must bestow upon their own dress, perhaps also upon that of their daughters, would alone go a great way towards achieving respectable results in art, or science, or literature, and does actually exhaust much of the time and mental power they might have to spare for either.[1] If it were possible that all this number of little practical interests (which are made great to them) should leave them either much leisure, or much energy and freedom of mind, to be devoted to art or speculation, they must have a much greater original supply of active faculty than the vast majority

---

[1] "It appears to be the same right turn of mind which enables a man to acquire the *truth*, or the just idea of what is right, in the ornaments, as in the more stable principles of art. It has still the same centre of perfection, though it is the centre of a smaller circle.—To illustrate this by the fashion of dress, in which there is allowed to be a good or bad taste. The component parts of dress are continually changing from great to little, from short to long; but the general form still remains: it is still the same general dress which is comparatively fixed, though on a very slender foundation; but it is on this which fashion must rest. He who invents with the most success, or dresses in the best taste, would probably, from the same sagacity employed to greater purposes, have discovered equal skill, or have formed the same correct taste, in the highest labours of art."—*Sir Joshua Reynolds's Discourses*, Disc. vii.

of men. But this is not all. Independently of the regular offices of life which devolve upon a woman, she is expected to have her time and faculties always at the disposal of everybody. If a man has not a profession to exempt him from such demands, still, if he has a pursuit, he offends nobody by devoting his time to it; occupation is received as a valid excuse for his not answering to every casual demand which may be made on him. Are a woman's occupations, especially her chosen and voluntary ones, ever regarded as excusing her from any of what are termed the calls of society? Scarcely are her most necessary and recognised duties allowed as an exemption. It requires an illness in the family, or something else out of the common way, to entitle her to give her own business the precedence over other people's amusement. She must always be at the beck and call of somebody, generally of everybody. If she has a study or a pursuit, she must snatch any short interval which accidentally occurs to be employed in it. A celebrated woman, in a work which I hope will some day be published, remarks truly that everything a woman does is done at odd times. Is it wonderful, then, if she does not attain the highest eminence in things which require consecutive attention, and the concentration on them of the chief interest of life? Such is philosophy, and such, above all, is art, in which, besides the devotion of the thoughts and feelings, the hand also must be kept in constant exercises to attain high skill.

There is another consideration to be added to all these. In the various arts and intellectual occupations, there is a degree of proficiency sufficient for living by it, and there is a higher degree on which depend the great productions which immortalise a name. To the attainment of the former, there are adequate motives in the case of all who follow the pursuit professionally: the other is hardly ever attained where there is not, or where there has not been at some period of life, an ardent desire of celebrity. Nothing less is commonly a sufficient stimulus to undergo the long and patient drudgery, which, in the case even of the greatest natural gifts, is absolutely required for great eminence in pursuits in which we already possess so many splendid memorials of the highest genius. Now, whether the cause be natural or artificial, women seldom have this eagerness for fame. Their ambition is generally confined within narrower bounds. The influence they seek is over those who immediately surround them. Their desire is to be liked, loved, or admired, by those whom they see with their eyes: and the proficiency in knowledge, arts, and accomplishments, which is sufficient for that, almost always contents them.   This is a trait of character which cannot be left out of the account in judging of women as they are.   I do not at all believe that it is inherent in women. It is only the natural result of their circumstances.   The love of fame in men is encouraged by education and opinion: to "scorn delights and live laborious days" for its sake, is accounted the part of "noble minds," even if spoken of as their "last infirmity," and is stimulated by the access which fame gives to all objects of ambition, including even the favour of women; while to women themselves all these objects are closed, and the desire of fame itself considered daring and unfeminine.   Besides, how could it be that a woman's interests should not be all concentrated upon the impressions made on those who come into her daily life, when society has ordained that all her duties should be to them, and has contrived that all her comforts should depend on them?   The natural desire of consideration from our fellow-creatures is as strong in a woman as in a man; but society has so ordered things that public consideration is, in all ordinary cases, only attainable by her through the consideration of her husband or of her male relations, while her private consideration is forfeited by making herself individually prominent, or appearing in any other character than that of an appendage to men.   Whoever is in the least capable of estimating the influence on the mind of the entire domestic and social position and the whole habit of a life, must easily recognise in that influence a complete explanation of nearly all the apparent differences between women and men, including the whole of those which imply any inferiority.

As for moral differences, considered as distinguished from intellectual, the distinction commonly drawn is to the advantage of women.   They are declared to be better than men; an empty compliment, which must provoke a bitter smile from every woman of spirit, since there is no other situation in life in which it is the established order, and considered quite natural and suitable, that the better should obey the worse.   If this piece of idle talk is good for anything, it is only as an admission by men, of the corrupting influence of power; for that is certainly the only truth which the fact, if it be a fact, either proves or illustrates.   And it *is* true that servitude, except when it actually brutalises, though corrupting to both, is less so to the slaves than to the slave-masters.   It is wholesomer for the moral nature to be restrained, even by arbitrary power, than to be allowed to exercise arbitrary power without restraint. Women, it is said, seldomer fall under the penal law—contribute a much smaller number of offenders to the criminal calendar, than men. I doubt not that the same thing may be said, with the same truth, of negro slaves. Those who are under the control of others cannot often commit crimes, unless at the command and for the purposes of their masters. I do not know a more signal instance of the blindness with which the world, including the herd of studious men, ignore and pass over all the influences of social circumstances, than their silly depreciation of the intellectual, and silly panegyrics on the moral, nature of women.

The complimentary dictum about women's superior moral goodness may be allowed to pair off with the disparaging one respecting their greater liability to moral bias. Women, we are told, are not capable of resisting their personal partialities: their judgment in grave affairs is warped by their sympathies and antipathies. Assuming it to be so, it is still to be proved that women are oftener misled by their personal feelings than men by their personal interests. The chief difference would seem in that case to be, that men are led from the course of duty and the public interest by their regard for themselves, women (not being allowed to have private interests of their own) by their regard for somebody else. It is also to be considered, that all the education which women receive from society inculcates on them the feeling that the individuals connected with them are the only ones to whom they owe any duty —the only ones whose interest they are called upon to care for; while, as far as education is concerned, they are left strangers even to the elementary ideas which are presupposed in any intelligent regard for larger interests or higher moral objects. The complaint against them resolves itself merely into this, that they fulfil only too faithfully the sole duty which they are taught, and almost the only one which they are permitted to practise.

The concessions of the privileged to the unprivileged are so seldom brought about by any better motive than the power of the unprivileged to extort them, that any arguments against the prerogative of sex are likely to be little attended to by the generality, as long as they are able to say to themselves that women do not complain of it. That fact certainly enables men to retain the unjust privilege some time longer; but does not render it less unjust. Exactly the same thing may be said of the women in the harem of an Oriental: they do not complain of not being allowed the freedom of European women. They think our women insufferably bold and unfeminine. How rarely it is that even men complain of the general order of society; and how much rarer still would such complaint be, if they did not know of any different order existing anywhere else. Women do not complain of the general lot of women; or rather they do, for plaintive elegies on it are very common in the writings of women, and were still more so as long as the lamentations could not be suspected of having any practical object. Their complaints are like the complaints which men make of the general unsatisfactoriness of human life; they are not meant to imply blame, or to plead for any change. But though women do not complain of the power of husbands, each complains of her own husband, or of the husbands of her friends. It is the same in all other cases of servitude, at least in the commencement of the emancipatory movement. The serfs did not at first complain of the power of their lords, but only of their tyranny. The commons began by claiming a few municipal privileges; they next asked an exemption for themselves from being taxed without their own consent; but they would at that time have thought it a great presumption to claim any share in the king's sovereign authority. The case of women is now the only case in which to rebel against established rules is still looked upon with the same eyes as was formerly a subject's claim to the right of rebelling against his king. A woman who joins in any movement which her husband disapproves, makes herself a martyr, without even being able to be an apostle, for the husband can legally put a stop to her apostleship. Women cannot be expected to devote themselves to the emancipation of women, until men in considerable number are prepared to join with them in the undertaking.

CHAPTER IV

THERE remains a question, not of less importance than those already discussed, and which will be asked the most importunately by those opponents whose conviction is somewhat shaken on the main point. What good are we to expect from the changes proposed in our customs and institutions? Would mankind be at all better off if women were free? If not, why disturb their minds, and attempt to make a social revolution in the name of an abstract right?

It is hardly to be expected that this question will be asked in respect to the change proposed in the condition of women in marriage. The sufferings, immoralities, evils of all sorts, produced in innumerable cases by the subjection of individual women to individual men, are far too terrible to be overlooked. Unthinking or uncandid persons, counting those cases alone which are extreme, or which attain publicity, may say that the evils are exceptional; but no one can be blind to their existence, nor, in many cases, to their intensity. And it is perfectly obvious that the abuse of the power cannot be very much checked while the power remains. It is a power given, or offered, not to good men, or to decently respectable men, but to all men; the most brutal, and the most criminal. There is no check but that of opinion, and such men are in general within the reach of no opinion but that of men like themselves. If such men did not brutally tyrannise over the one human being whom the law compels to bear everything from them, society must already have reached a paradisiacal state. There could be no need any longer of laws to curb men's vicious propensities. Astræa must not only have returned to earth, but the heart of the worst man must have become her temple. The law of servitude in marriage is a monstrous contradiction to all the principles of the modern world, and to all the experience through which those principles have been slowly and painfully worked out. It is the sole case, now that negro slavery has been abolished, in which a human being in the plenitude of every faculty is delivered up to the tender mercies of another human being, in the hope forsooth that this other will use the power

79

solely for the good of the person subjected to it. Marriage is the only actual bondage known to our law. There remain no legal slaves, except the mistress of every house.

It is not, therefore, on this part of the subject, that the question is likely to be asked, *Cui bono ?* We may be told that the evil would outweigh the good, but the reality of the good admits of no dispute. In regard, however, to the larger question, the removal of women's disabilities—their recognition as the equals of men in all that belongs to citizenship—the opening to them of all honourable employments, and of the training and education which qualifies for those employments — there are many persons for whom it is not enough that the inequality has no just or legitimate defence; they require to be told what express advantage would be obtained by abolishing it.

To which let me first answer, the advantage of having the most universal and pervading of all human relations regulated by justice instead of injustice. The vast amount of this gain to human nature, it is hardly possible, by any explanation or illustration, to place in a stronger light than it is placed by the bare statement, to anyone who attaches a moral meaning to words. All the selfish propensities, the self-worship, the unjust self-preference, which exist among mankind, have their source and root in, and derive their principal nourishment from, the present constitution of the relation between men and women. Think what it is to a boy, to grow up to manhood in the belief that without any merit or any exertion of his own, though he may be the most frivolous and empty or the most ignorant and stolid of mankind, by the mere fact of being born a male he is by right the superior of all and every one of an entire half of the human race: including probably some whose real superiority to himself he has daily or hourly occasion to feel; but even if in his whole conduct he habitually follows a woman's guidance, still, if he is a fool, she thinks that of course she is not, and cannot be, equal in ability and judgment to himself; and if he is not a fool, he does worse—he sees that she is superior to him, and believes that, notwithstanding her superiority, he is entitled to command and she is bound to obey. What must be the effect on his character, of this lesson? And men of the cultivated classes are often not aware how deeply it sinks into the immense majority of male minds. For, among right-feeling and well-bred people, the inequality is kept as much as possible out of sight; above all, out of sight of the children. As much obedience is required from boys to their mother as to their father: they are not permitted to domineer over their sisters, nor are they accustomed to see these postponed to them, but the contrary; the compensations of the chivalrous feeling being made prominent, while the servitude which requires them is kept in the background. Well brought-up youths in the higher classes thus often escape the bad influences of the situation in their early years, and only experience them when, arrived at manhood, they fall under the dominion of facts as they really exist. Such people are little aware, when a boy is differently brought up, how early the notion of his inherent superiority to a girl arises in his mind; how it grows with his growth and strengthens with his strength; how it is inoculated by one schoolboy upon another; how early the youth thinks himself superior to his mother, owing her perhaps forbearance, but no real respect; and how sublime and sultan-like a sense of superiority he feels, above all, over the woman whom he honours by admitting her to a partnership of his life. Is it imagined that all this does not pervert the whole manner of existence of the man, both as an individual and as a social being? It is an exact parallel to the feeling of a hereditary king that he is excellent above others by being born a king, or a noble by being born a noble. The relation between husband and wife is very like that between lord and vassal, except that the wife is held to more unlimited obedience than the vassal was. However the vassal's character may have been affected, for better and for worse, by his subordination, who can help seeing that the lord's was affected greatly for the worse? whether he was led to believe that his vassals were really superior to himself, or to feel that he was placed in command over people as good as himself, for no merits or labours of his own, but merely for having, as Figaro says, taken the trouble to be born. The self-worship of the monarch, or of the feudal superior, is matched by the self-worship of the male. Human beings do not grow up from childhood in the possession of unearned distinctions, without pluming themselves upon them. Those whom privileges not acquired by their merit, and which they feel to be disproportioned to it, inspire with additional humility, are always the few, and the best few. The rest are only inspired with pride, and the worst sort of pride, that which values itself upon accidental advantages, not of its own achieving. Above all, when the feeling of being raised above the whole of the other sex is combined with personal authority over one individual among them; the situation, if a school of conscientious and affectionate forbearance to those whose strongest points of character are conscience and affection, is to men of another quality a regularly constituted academy or gymnasium for training them in arrogance and overbearingness; which vices, if curbed by the certainty of resistance in their intercourse with other men, their equals, break out towards all who are in a position to be obliged to tolerate them, and often revenge themselves upon the unfortunate wife for the involuntary restraint which they are obliged to submit to elsewhere.

The example afforded, and the education given to the sentiments, by laying the foundation of domestic existence upon a relation contradictory to the first principles of social justice, must, from the very nature of man, have a perverting influence of such magnitude, that it is hardly possible with our present experience to raise our imaginations to the conception of so great a change for the better as would be made by its removal. All that education and civilisation are doing to efface the influences on character of the law of force, and replace them by those of justice, remains merely on the surface, as long as the citadel of the enemy is not attacked. The principle of the modern movement in morals and politics, is that conduct, and conduct alone, entitles to respect: that not what men are, but what they do, constitutes their claim to deference; that, above all, merit, and not birth, is the only rightful claim to power and authority. If no authority, not in its nature temporary, were allowed to one human being over another, society would not be employed in building up propensities with one hand which it has to curb with the other. The child would really, for the first time in man's existence on earth, be trained in the way he should go, and when he was old there would be a chance that he would not depart from it. But so long as the right of the strong to power over the weak rules in the very heart of society, the attempt to make the equal right of the weak the principle of its outward actions will always be an uphill struggle; for the law of justice, which is also that of Christianity, will never get possession of men's inmost sentiments; they will be working against it, even when bending to it.

The second benefit to be expected from giving to women the free use of their faculties, by leaving them the free choice of their employments, and opening to them the same field of occupation and the same prizes and encouragements as to other human beings, would be that of doubling the mass of mental faculties available for the higher service of humanity. Where there is now one person qualified to benefit mankind and promote the general improvement, as a public teacher, or an administrator of some branch of public or social affairs, there would then be a chance of two. Mental superiority of any kind is at present everywhere so much below the demand; there is such a deficiency of persons competent to do excellently anything which it requires any considerable amount of ability to do; that the loss to the world, by refusing to make use of one-half of the whole quantity of talent it possesses, is extremely serious. It is true that this amount of mental power is not totally lost. Much of it is employed, and would in any case be employed, in domestic management, and in the few other occupations open to women; and from the remainder indirect benefit is in many individual cases obtained, through the personal influence of individual women over individual men. But these benefits are partial; their range is extremely circumscribed; and if they must be admitted, on the one hand, as a deduction from the amount of fresh social power that would be acquired by giving freedom to one-half of the whole sum of human intellect, there must be added, on the other, the benefit of the stimulus that would be given to the intellect of men by the competition; or (to use a more true expression) by the necessity that would be imposed on them of deserving precedency before they could expect to obtain it.

This great accession to the intellectual power of the species, and to the amount of intellect available for the good management of its affairs, would be obtained, partly, through the better and more complete intellectual education of women, which would then improve *pari passu* with that of men. Women in general would be brought up equally capable of understanding business, public affairs, and the higher matters of speculation, with men in the same class of society; and the select few of the one as well as of the other sex, who were qualified not only to comprehend what is done or thought by others, but to think or do something considerable themselves, would meet with the same facilities for improving and training their capacities in the one sex as in the other. In this way, the widening of the sphere of action for women would operate for good, by raising their education to the level of that of men, and making the one participate in all improvements made in the other. But independently of this, the mere breaking down of the barrier would of itself have an educational virtue of the highest worth. The mere getting rid of the idea that all the wider subjects of thought and action, all the things which are of general and not solely of private interest, are men's business, from which women are to be warned off—positively interdicted from most of it, coldly tolerated in the little which is allowed them—the mere consciousness a woman would then have of being a human being like any other, entitled to choose her pursuits, urged or invited by the same inducements as anyone else to interest herself in whatever is interesting to human beings, entitled to exert the share of influence on all human concerns which belongs to an individual opinion, whether she attempted actual participation in them or not—this alone would effect an immense expansion of the faculties of women, as well as enlargement of the range of their moral sentiments.

Besides the addition to the amount of individual talent available for the conduct of human affairs, which certainly are not at present so abundantly provided in that respect that they can afford to dispense with one-half of what nature proffers; the opinion of women would then possess a more beneficial, rather than a greater, influence upon the general mass of human belief and sentiment. I say a more beneficial, rather than a greater influence; for the influence of women over the general tone of opinion has always, or at least from the earliest known period, been very considerable. The influence of mothers on the early character of their sons, and the desire of young men to recommend themselves to young women, have in all recorded times been important agencies in the formation of character, and have determined some of the chief steps in the progress of civilisation. Even in the Homeric age, αἰδὼς towards the Τρωάδας ἑλκεσιπέπλους is an acknowledged and powerful motive of action in the great Hector. The moral influence of women has had two modes of operation. First, it has been a softening influence. Those who were most liable to be the victims of violence, have naturally tended as much as they could towards limiting its sphere and mitigating its excesses. Those who were not taught to fight, have naturally inclined in favour of any other mode of settling differences rather than that of fighting. In general, those who have been the greatest sufferers by the indulgence of selfish passion, have been the most earnest supporters of any moral law which offered a means of bridling passion. Women were powerfully instrumental in inducing the northern conquerors to adopt the creed of Christianity, a creed so much more favourable to women than any that preceded it. The conversion of the Anglo-Saxons and of the Franks may be said to have been begun by the wives of Ethelbert and Clovis. The other mode in which the effect of women's opinion has been conspicuous, is by giving a powerful stimulus to those qualities in men, which, not being themselves trained in, it was necessary for them that they should find in their protectors. Courage, and the military virtues generally, have at all times been greatly indebted to the desire which men felt of being admired by women: and the stimulus reaches far beyond this one class of eminent qualities, since, by a very natural effect of their position, the best passport to the admiration and favour of women has always been to be thought highly of by men. From the combination of the two kinds of moral influence thus exercised by women, arose the spirit of chivalry: the peculiarity of which is, to aim at combining the highest standard of the warlike qualities with the cultivation of a totally different class of virtues—those of gentleness, generosity, and self-abnegation, towards the non-military and defenceless classes generally, and a special submission and worship directed towards women; who were distinguished from the other defenceless classes by the high rewards which they had it in their power voluntarily to bestow on those who endeavoured to earn their favour, instead of extorting their subjection. Though the practice of chivalry fell even more sadly short of its theoretic standard than practice generally falls below theory, it remains one of the most precious monuments of the moral history of our race; as a remarkable instance of a concerted and organised attempt by a most disorganised and distracted society, to raise up and carry into practice a moral ideal greatly in advance of its social condition and institutions; so much so as to have been completely frustrated in the main object, yet never entirely inefficacious, and which has left a most sensible, and for the most part a highly valuable impress on the ideas and feelings of all subsequent times.

The chivalrous ideal is the acme of the influence of women's sentiments on the moral cultivation of mankind: and if women are to remain in their subordinate situation, it were greatly to be lamented that the chivalrous standard should have passed away, for it is the only one at all capable of mitigating the demoralising influences of that position. But the changes in the general state of the species rendered inevitable the substitution of a totally different ideal of morality for the chivalrous one. Chivalry was the attempt to infuse moral elements into a state of society in which everything depended for good or evil on individual prowess, under the softening influences of individual delicacy and generosity. In modern societies, all things, even in the military department of affairs, are decided, not by individual effort, but by the combined operations of numbers; while the main occupation of society has changed from fighting to business, from military to industrial life. The exigencies of the new life are no more exclusive of the virtues of generosity than those of the old, but it no longer entirely depends on them. The main foundations of the moral life of modern times must be justice and prudence; the respect of each for the rights of every other, and the ability of each to take care of himself. Chivalry left without legal check all forms of wrong which reigned unpunished throughout society; it only encouraged a few to do right in preference to wrong, by the direction it gave to the instruments of praise and admiration. But the real dependence of morality must always be upon its penal sanctions—its power to deter from evil. The security of society cannot rest on merely rendering honour to right, a motive so comparatively weak in all but a few, and which on very many does not operate at all. Modern society is able to repress wrong through all departments of life, by a fit exertion of the superior strength which civilisation has given it, and thus to render the existence of the weaker members of society (no longer defenceless but protected by law) tolerable to them, without reliance on the chivalrous feelings of those who are in a position to tyrannise. The beauties and graces of the chivalrous character are still what they were, but the rights of the weak, and the general comfort of human life, now rest on a far surer and steadier support; or rather, they do so in every relation of life except the conjugal.

At present the moral influence of women is no less real, but it is no longer of so marked and definite a character: it has more nearly merged in the general influence of public opinion. Both through the contagion of sympathy, and through the desire of men to shine in the eyes of women, their feelings have great effect in keeping alive what remains of the chivalrous ideal—in fostering the sentiments and continuing the traditions of spirit and generosity. In these points of character, their standard is higher than that of men; in the quality of justice, somewhat lower. As regards the relations of private life it may be said generally, that their influence is, on the whole, encouraging to the softer virtues, discouraging to the sterner: though the statement must be taken with all the modifications dependent on individual character. In the chief of the greater trials to which virtue is subject in the concerns of life—the conflict between interest and principle—the tendency of women's influence is of a very mixed character. When the principle involved happens to be one of the very few which the course of their religious or moral education has strongly impressed upon themselves, they are potent auxiliaries to virtue: and their husbands and sons are often prompted by them to acts of abnegation which they never would have been capable of without that stimulus. But, with the present education and position of women, the moral principles which have been impressed on them cover but a comparatively small part of the field of virtue, and are, more-over, principally negative; forbidding particular acts, but having little to do with the general direction of the thoughts and purposes. I am afraid it must be said, that disinterestedness in the general conduct of life—the devotion of the energies to purposes which hold out no promise of private advantages to the family—is very seldom encouraged or supported by women's influence. It is small blame to them that they discourage objects of which they have not learnt to see the advantage, and which withdraw their men from them, and from the interests of the family. But the consequence is that women's influence is often anything but favourable to public virtue.

Women have, however, some share of influence in giving the tone to public moralities since their sphere of action has been a little widened, and since a considerable number of them have occupied themselves practically in the promotion of objects reaching beyond their own family and household. The influence of women counts for a great deal in two of the most marked features of modern European life—its aversion to war, and its addiction to philanthropy. Excellent characteristics both; but unhappily, if the influence of women is valuable in the en-couragement it gives to these feelings in general, in the particular applications the direction it gives to them is at least as often mischievous as useful. In the philanthropic department more particularly, the two provinces chiefly cultivated by women are religious proselytism and charity. Religious proselytism at home, is but another word for embittering of religious ani-mosities: abroad, it is usually a blind running at an object, without either knowing or heeding the fatal mischiefs—fatal to the religious object itself as well as to all other desirable objects —which may be produced by the means employed. As for charity, it is a matter in which the immediate effect on the persons directly concerned, and the ultimate consequence to the general good, are apt to be at complete war with one another: while the education given to women—an education of the sentiments rather than of the understanding—and the habit inculcated by their whole life, of looking to immediate effects on persons, and not to remote effects on classes of persons— make them both unable to see, and unwilling to admit, the ultimate evil tendency of any form of charity or philanthropy which commends itself to their sympathetic feelings. The great and continually increasing mass of unenlightened and short-sighted benevolence, which, taking the care of people's lives out of their own hands, and relieving them from the disagreeable consequences of their own acts, saps the very foundations of the self-respect, self-help, and self-control which are the essential conditions both of individual prosperity and of social virtue— this waste of resources and of benevolent feelings in doing harm instead of good, is immensely swelled by women's contributions, and stimulated by their influence. Not that this is a mistake likely to be made by women, where they have actually the practical management of schemes of beneficence. It sometimes happens that women who administer public charities—with that insight into present fact, and especially into the minds and feelings of those with whom they are in immediate con-tact, in which women generally excel men—recognise in the clearest manner the demoralising influence of the alms given or the help afforded, and could give lessons on the subject to many a male political economist. But women who only give their money, and are not brought face to face with the effects it produces, how can they be expected to foresee them? A woman born to the present lot of women, and content with it, how should she appreciate the value of self-dependence? She is not self-dependent; she is not taught self-dependence; her destiny is to receive everything from others, and why should what is good enough for her be bad for the poor? Her familiar notions of good are of blessings descending from a superior. She forgets that she is not free, and that the poor are; that if what they need is given to them unearned, they cannot be compelled to earn it: that everybody cannot be taken care of by everybody, but there must be some motive to induce people to take care of themselves; and that to be helped to help themselves, if they are physically capable of it, is the only charity which proves to be charity in the end.

These considerations show how usefully the part which

women take in the formation of general opinion, would be modified for the better by that more enlarged instruction, and practical conversancy with the things which their opinions influence, that would necessarily arise from their social and political emancipation. But the improvement it would work through the influence they exercise, each in her own family, would be still more remarkable.

It is often said that in the classes most exposed to temptation, a man's wife and children tend to keep him honest and respectable, both by the wife's direct influence, and by the concern he feels for their future welfare. This may be so, and no doubt often is so, with those who are more weak than wicked; and this beneficial influence would be preserved and strengthened under equal laws; it does not depend on the woman's servitude, but is, on the contrary, diminished by the disrespect which the inferior class of men always at heart feel towards those who are subject to their power. But when we ascend higher in the scale, we come among a totally different set of moving forces. The wife's influence tends, as far as it goes, to prevent the husband from falling below the common standard of approbation of the country. It tends quite as strongly to hinder him from rising above it. The wife is the auxiliary of the common public opinion. A man who is married to a woman his inferior in intelligence, finds her a perpetual dead weight, or, worse than a dead weight, a drag, upon every aspiration of his to be better than public opinion requires him to be. It is hardly possible for one who is in these bonds, to attain exalted virtue. If he differs in his opinion from the mass—if he sees truths which have not yet dawned upon them, or if, feeling in his heart truths which they nominally recognise, he would like to act up to those truths more conscientiously than the generality of mankind—to all such thoughts and desires, marriage is the heaviest of drawbacks, unless he be so fortunate as to have a wife as much above the common level as he himself is.

For, in the first place, there is always some sacrifice of personal interest required; either of social consequence, or of pecuniary means; perhaps the risk of even the means of subsistence. These sacrifices and risks he may be willing to encounter for himself; but he will pause before he imposes them on his family. And his family in this case means his wife and daughters; for he always hopes that his sons will feel as he feels himself, and that what he can do without, they will do without, willingly, in the same cause. But his daughters—their marriage may depend upon it: and his wife, who is unable to enter into or understand the objects for which these sacrifices are made—who, if she thought them worth any sacrifice, would think so on trust, and solely for his sake—who could participate in none of the enthusiasm or the self-approbation he himself may feel, while the things which he is disposed to sacrifice are all in all to her; will not the best and most unselfish man hesitate the longest before bringing on her this consequence? If it be not the comforts of life, but only social consideration, that is at stake, the burthen upon his conscience and feelings is still very severe. Whoever has a wife and children has given hostages to Mrs. Grundy. The approbation of that potentate may be a matter of indifference to him, but it is of great importance to his wife. The man himself may be above opinion, or may find sufficient compensation in the opinion of those of his own way of thinking. But to the women connected with him, he can offer no compensation. The almost invariable tendency of the wife to place her influence in the same scale with social consideration, is sometimes made a reproach to women, and represented as a peculiar trait of feebleness and childishness of character in them: surely with great injustice. Society makes the whole life of a woman, in the easy classes, a continued self-sacrifice; it exacts from her an unremitting restraint of the whole of her natural inclinations, and the sole return it makes to her for what often deserves the name of a martyrdom, is consideration. Her consideration is inseparably connected with that of her husband, and after paying the full price for it, she finds that she is to lose it, for no reason of which she can feel the cogency. She has sacrificed her whole life to it, and her husband will not sacrifice to it a whim, a freak, an eccentricity; something not recognised or allowed for by the world, and which the world will agree with her in thinking a folly, if it thinks no worse! The dilemma is hardest upon that very meritorious class of men, who, without possessing talents which qualify them to make a figure among those with whom they agree in opinion, hold their opinion from conviction, and feel bound in honour and conscience to serve it, by making profession of their belief, and giving their time, labour, and means, to anything undertaken in its behalf. The worst case of all is when such men happen to be of a rank and position which of itself neither gives them, nor excludes them from, what is considered the best society; when their admission to it depends mainly on what is thought of them personally—and however unexceptionable their breeding and habits, their being identified with opinions and public conduct unacceptable to those who give the tone to society would operate as an effectual exclusion. Many a woman flatters herself (nine times out of ten quite erroneously) that nothing prevents her and her husband from moving in the highest society of her neighbourhood—society in which others well known to her, and in the same class of life, mix freely—except that her husband is unfortunately a Dissenter, or has the reputation of mingling in low radical politics. That it is, she thinks, which hinders George from getting a commission or a place, Caroline from making an advantageous match, and prevents her and her husband from obtaining invitations, perhaps honours, which, for aught she sees, they are as well entitled to as some folks. With such an influence in every house, either exerted actively, or operating all the more powerfully for not being asserted, is it any wonder that people in general are kept down in that mediocrity of respectability which is becoming a marked characteristic of modern times?

There is another very injurious aspect in which the effect, not of women's disabilities directly, but of the broad line of difference which those disabilities create between the education and character of a woman and that of a man, requires to be considered. Nothing can be more unfavourable to that union of thoughts and inclinations which is the ideal of married life. Intimate society between people radically dissimilar to one another, is an idle dream. Unlikeness may attract, but it is likeness which retains; and in proportion to the likeness is the suitability of the individuals to give each other a happy life. While women are so unlike men, it is not wonderful that selfish men should feel the need of arbitrary power in their own hands, to arrest *in limine* the life-long conflict of inclinations, by deciding every question on the side of their own preference. When people are extremely unlike, there can be no real identity of interest. Very often there is conscientious difference of opinion between married people, on the highest points of duty. Is there any reality in the marriage union where this takes place? Yet it is not uncommon anywhere, when the woman has any earnestness of character; and it is a very general case indeed in Catholic countries, when she is supported in her dissent by the only other authority to which she is taught to bow, the priest. With the usual barefacedness of power not accustomed to find itself disputed, the influence of priests over women is attacked by Protestant and Liberal writers, less for being bad in itself, than because it is a rival authority to the husband, and raises up a revolt against his infallibility. In England, similar differences occasionally exist when an Evangelical wife has allied herself with a husband of a different quality; but in general this source at least of dissension is got rid of, by reducing the minds of women to such a nullity, that they have no opinions but those of Mrs. Grundy, or those which the husband tells them to have. When there is no difference of opinion, differences merely of taste may be sufficient to detract greatly from the happiness of married life. And though it may stimulate the amatory propensities of men, it does not conduce to married happiness, to exaggerate by differences of education whatever may be the native differences of the sexes. If the married pair are well-bred and well-behaved people, they tolerate each other's tastes; but is mutual toleration what people look forward to, when they enter into marriage? These differences of inclination will naturally make their wishes different, if not restrained by affection or duty, as to almost all domestic questions which arise. What a difference there must be in the society which the two persons will wish to frequent, or be frequented by! Each will desire associates who share their own tastes: the persons agreeable to one, will be indifferent or positively disagreeable to the other; yet there can be none who are not common to both, for married people do not now live in different parts of the house and have totally different visiting lists, as in the reign of Louis XV. They cannot help having different wishes as to the bringing up of the children: each will wish to see reproduced in them their own tastes and sentiments: and there is either a compromise, and only a half-satisfaction to either, or the wife has to yield—often with bitter suffering; and, with or without intention, her occult influence continues to counterwork the husband's purposes.

It would of course be extreme folly to suppose that these differences of feeling and inclination only exist because women are brought up differently from men, and that there would not be differences of taste under any imaginable circumstances. But there is nothing beyond the mark in saying that the distinction in bringing up immensely aggravates those differences, and renders them wholly inevitable. While women are brought up as they are, a man and a woman will but rarely find in one another real agreement of tastes and wishes as to daily life. They will generally have to give it up as hopeless, and renounce the attempt to have, in the intimate associate of their daily life, that *idem velle, idem nolle,* which is the recognised bond of any society that is really such: or if the man succeeds in obtaining it, he does so by choosing a woman who is so complete a nullity that she has no *velle* or *nolle* at all, and is as ready to comply with one thing as another if anybody tells her to do so. Even this calculation is apt to fail; dullness and want of spirit are not always a guarantee of the submission which is so confidently expected from them. But if they were, is this the ideal of marriage? What, in this case, does the man obtain by it, except an upper servant, a nurse, or a mistress? On the contrary, when each of two persons, instead of being a nothing, is a something; when they are attached to one another, and are not too much unlike to begin with; the constant partaking in the same things, assisted by their sympathy, draws out the latent capacities of each for being interested in the things which were at first interesting only to the other; and works a gradual assimilation of the tastes and characters to one another, partly by the insensible modification of each, but more by a real enriching of the two natures, each acquiring the tastes and capacities of the other in addition to its own. This often happens between two friends of the same sex, who are much associated in their daily life: and it would be a common, if not the commonest, case in marriage, did not the totally different bringing up of the two sexes make it next to an impossibility to form a really well-assorted union. Were this remedied, whatever differences there might still be in individual tastes, there would at least be, as a general rule, complete unity and unanimity as to the great objects of life. When the two persons both care for great objects, and are a help and encouragement to each other in whatever regards these, the minor matters on which their tastes may differ are not all-important to them; and there is a foundation for solid friendship, of an enduring character, more likely than anything else to make it, through the whole of life, a greater pleasure to each to give pleasure to the other, than to receive it.

I have considered, thus far, the effects on the pleasures and benefits of the marriage union which depend on the mere unlikeness between the wife and the husband: but the evil tendency is prodigiously aggravated when the unlikeness is inferiority. Mere unlikeness, when it only means difference of good qualities, may be more a benefit in the way of mutual improvement, than a drawback from comfort. When each emulates, and desires and endeavours to acquire, the other's peculiar qualities the difference does not produce diversity of interest, but increased identity of it, and makes each still more valuable to the other. But when one is much the inferior of the two in mental ability and cultivation, and is not actively attempting by the other's aid to rise to the other's level, the whole influence of the connexion upon the development of the superior of the two is deteriorating: and still more so in a tolerably happy marriage than in an unhappy one. It is not with impunity that the superior in intellect shuts himself up with an inferior, and elects that inferior for his chosen, and sole completely intimate, associate. Any society which is not improving, is deteriorating: and the more so, the closer and more familiar it is. Even a really superior man almost always begins to deteriorate when he is habitually (as the phrase is) king of his company: and in his most habitual company the husband who has a wife inferior to him is always so. While his self-satisfaction is incessantly ministered to on the one hand, on the other he insensibly imbibes the modes of feeling, and of looking at things, which belong to a more vulgar or a more limited mind than his own. This evil differs from many of those which have hitherto been dwelt on, by being an increasing one. The association of men with women in daily life is much closer and more complete than it ever was before. Men's life is more domestic. Formerly, their pleasures and chosen occupations were among men, and in men's company: their wives had but a fragment of their lives. At the present time, the progress of civilisation, and the turn of opinion against the rough amusements and convivial excesses which formerly occupied most men in their hours of relaxation—together with (it must be said) the improved tone of modern feeling as to the reciprocity of duty which binds the husband towards the wife—have thrown the man very much more upon home and its inmates, for his personal and social pleasures: while the kind and degree of improvement which has been made in women's education, has made them in some degree capable of being his companions in ideas and mental taste, while leaving them, in most cases, still hopelessly inferior to him. His desire of mental communion is thus in general satisfied by a communion from which he learns nothing. An unimproving and unstimulating companionship is substituted for (what he might otherwise have been obliged to seek) the society of his equals in powers and his fellows in the higher pursuits. We see, accordingly, that young men of the greatest promise generally cease to improve as soon as they marry, and, not improving, inevitably degenerate. If the wife does not push the husband forward, she always holds him back. He ceases to care for what she does not care for; he no longer desires, and ends by disliking and shunning, society congenial to his former aspirations, and which would now shame his falling-off from them; his higher faculties both of mind and heart cease to be called into activity. And this change coinciding with the new and selfish interests which are created by the family, after a few years he differs in no material respect from those who have never had wishes for anything but the common vanities and the common pecuniary objects.

What marriage may be in the case of two persons of cultivated faculties, identical in opinions and purposes, between whom there exists that best kind of equality, similarity of powers and capacities with reciprocal superiority in them—so that each can enjoy the luxury of looking up to the other, and can have alternately the pleasure of leading and of being led in the path of development—I will not attempt to describe. To those who can conceive it, there is no need; to those who cannot, it would appear the dream of an enthusiast. But I maintain, with the profoundest conviction, that this, and this only, is the ideal of marriage; and that all opinions, customs, and institutions which favour any other notion of it, or turn the conceptions and aspirations connected with it into any other direction, by whatever pretences they may be coloured, are relics of primitive barbarism. The moral regeneration of mankind will only really commence, when the most fundamental of the social relations is placed under the rule of equal justice, and when human beings learn to cultivate their strongest sympathy with an equal in rights and in cultivation.

Thus far, the benefits which it has appeared that the world would gain by ceasing to make sex a disqualification for privileges and a badge of subjection, are social rather than individual; consisting in an increase of the general fund of thinking and acting power, and an improvement in the general conditions of the association of men with women. But it would be a grievous understatement of the case to omit the most direct benefit of all, the unspeakable gain in private happiness to the liberated half of the species; the difference to them between a life of subjection to the will of others, and a life of rational freedom. After the primary necessities of food and raiment, freedom is the first and strongest want of human nature. While mankind are lawless, their desire is for lawless freedom. When they have learnt to understand the meaning of duty and the value of reason, they incline more and more to be guided and restrained by these in the exercise of their freedom; but they do not therefore desire freedom less; they do not become disposed to accept the will of other people as the representative and interpreter of those guiding principles. On the contrary, the communities in which the reason has been most cultivated, and in which the idea of social duty has been most powerful, are those which have most strongly asserted the freedom of action of the individual—the liberty of each to govern his conduct by his own feelings of duty, and by such laws and social restraints as his own conscience can subscribe to.

He who would rightly appreciate the worth of personal independence as an element of happiness, should consider the value he himself puts upon it as an ingredient of his own. There is no subject on which there is a greater habitual difference of judgment between a man judging for himself, and the same man judging for other people. When he hears others complaining that they are not allowed freedom of action—that their own will has not sufficient influence in the regulation of their affairs—his inclination is, to ask, what are their grievances? what positive damage they sustain? and in what respect they consider their affairs to be mismanaged? and if they fail to make out, in answer to these questions, what appears to him a sufficient case, he turns a deaf ear, and regards their complaint as the fanciful querulousness of people whom nothing reasonable will satisfy. But he has a quite different standard of judgment when he is deciding for himself. Then, the most unexceptionable administration of his interests by a tutor set over him, does not satisfy his feelings: his personal exclusion from the deciding authority appears itself the greatest grievance of all, rendering it superfluous even to enter into the question of mismanagement. It is the same with nations. What citizen of a free country would listen to any offers of good and skilful administration, in return for the abdication of freedom? Even if he could believe that good and skilful administration can exist among a people ruled by a will not their own, would not the consciousness of working out their own destiny under their own moral responsibility be a compensation to his feelings for great rudeness and imperfection in the details of public affairs? Let him rest assured that whatever he feels on this point, women feel in a fully equal degree. Whatever has been said or written, from the time of Herodotus to the present, of the ennobling influence of free government—the nerve and spring which it gives to all the faculties, the larger and higher objects which it presents to the intellect and feelings, the more unselfish public spirit, and calmer and broader views of duty, that it engenders, and the generally loftier platform on which it elevates the individual as a moral, spiritual, and social being—is every particle as true of women as of men. Are these things no important part of individual happiness? Let any man call to mind what he himself felt on emerging from boyhood—from the tutelage and control of even loved and affectionate elders—and entering upon the responsibilities of manhood. Was it not like the physical effect of taking off a heavy weight, or releasing him from obstructive, even if not otherwise painful, bonds? Did he not feel twice as much alive, twice as much a human being, as before? And does he imagine that women have none of these feelings? But it is a striking fact, that the satisfactions and mortifications of personal pride, though all in all to most men when the case is their own, have less allowance made for them in the case of other people, and are less listened to as a ground or a justification of conduct, than any other natural human feelings; perhaps because men compliment them in their own case with the names of so many other qualities, that they are seldom conscious how mighty an influence these feelings exercise in their own lives. No less large and powerful is their part, we may assure ourselves, in the lives and feelings of women. Women are schooled into suppressing them in their most natural and most healthy direction, but the internal principle remains, in a different outward form. An active and energetic mind, if denied liberty, will seek for power: refused the command of itself, it will assert its personality by attempting to control others. To allow to any human beings no existence of their own but what depends on others, is giving far too high a premium on bending others to their purposes. Where liberty cannot be hoped for, and power can, power becomes the grand object of human desire; those to whom others will not leave the undisturbed management of their own affairs, will compensate themselves, if they can, by meddling for their own purposes with the affairs of others. Hence also women's passion for personal beauty, and dress and display; and all the evils that flow from it, in the way of mischievous luxury and social immorality. The love of power and the love of liberty are in eternal antagonism. Where there is least liberty, the passion for power is the most ardent and unscrupulous. The desire of power over others can only cease to be a depraving agency among mankind, when each of them individually is able to do without it: which can only be where respect for liberty in the personal concerns of each is an established principle.

But it is not only through the sentiment of personal dignity, that the free direction and disposal of their own faculties is a source of individual happiness, and to be fettered and restricted in it, a source of unhappiness, to human beings, and not least to women. There is nothing, after disease, indigence, and guilt, so fatal to the pleasurable enjoyment of life as the want of a worthy outlet for the active faculties. Women who have the cares of a family, and while they have the cares of a family, have this outlet, and it generally suffices for them: but what of the greatly increasing number of women, who have had no opportunity of exercising the vocation which they are mocked by telling them is their proper one? What of the women whose children have been lost to them by death or distance, or have grown up, married, and formed homes of their own? There are abundant examples of men who, after a life engrossed by business, retire with a competency to the enjoyment, as they hope, of rest, but to whom, as they are unable to acquire new interests and excitements that can replace the old, the change to a life of inactivity brings ennui, melancholy, and premature death. Yet no one thinks of the parallel case of so many worthy and devoted women, who, having paid what they are told is their debt to society—having brought up a family blamelessly to manhood and womanhood—having kept a house as long as they had a house needing to be kept—are deserted by the sole occupation for which they have fitted themselves; and remain with undiminished activity but with no employment for it, unless perhaps a daughter or daughter-in-law is willing to abdicate in their favour the discharge of the same functions in her younger household. Surely a hard lot for the old age of those who have worthily discharged, as long as it was given to them to discharge, what the world accounts their only social duty. Of such women, and of those others to whom this duty has not been committed at all—many of whom pine through life with the consciousness of thwarted vocations, and activities which are not suffered to expand—the only resources, speaking generally, are religion and charity. But their religion, though it may be one of feeling, and of ceremonial observance, cannot be a religion of action, unless in the form of charity. For charity many of them are by nature admirably fitted; but to practise it usefully, or even without doing mischief, requires the education, the manifold preparation, the knowledge and the thinking powers, of a skilful administrator. There are few of the administrative functions of government for which a person would not be fit, who is fit to bestow charity usefully. In this as in other cases (pre-eminently in that of the education of children), the duties permitted to women cannot be performed properly, without their being trained for duties which, to the great loss of society, are not permitted to them. And here let me notice the singular way in which the question of women's disabilities is frequently presented to view, by those who find it easier to draw a ludicrous picture of what they do not like, than to answer the arguments for it. When it is suggested that women's executive capacities and prudent counsels might sometimes be found valuable in affairs of State, these lovers of fun hold up to the ridicule of the world, as sitting in Parliament or in the Cabinet, girls in their teens, or young wives of two or three and twenty, transported bodily, exactly as they are, from the drawing-room to the House of Commons. They forget that males are not usually selected at this early age for a seat in Parliament, or for responsible political functions. Common sense would tell them that if such trusts were confided to women, it would be to such as having no special vocation for married life, or preferring another employment of their faculties (as many women even now prefer to marriage some of the few honourable occupations within their reach), have spent the best years of their youth in attempting to qualify themselves for the pursuits in which they desire to engage; or still more frequently perhaps, widows or wives of forty or fifty, by whom the knowledge of life and faculty of government which they have acquired in their families, could by the aid of appropriate studies be made available on a less contracted scale. There is no country of Europe in which the ablest men have not frequently experienced, and keenly appreciated, the value of the advice and help of clever and experienced women of the world, in the attainment both of private and of public objects; and there are important matters of public administration to which few men are equally competent with such women; among others, the detailed control of expenditure. But what we are now discussing is not the need which society has of the services of women in public business, but the dull and hopeless life to which it so often condemns them, by forbidding them to exercise the practical abilities which many of them are conscious of, in any wider field than one which to some of them never was, and to others is no longer, open. If there is anything vitally important to the happiness of human beings, it is that they should relish their habitual pursuit. This requisite of an enjoyable life is very imperfectly granted, or altogether denied, to a large part of mankind; and by its absence many a life is a failure, which is provided, in appearance, with every requisite of success. But if circumstances which society is not yet skilful enough to overcome, render such failures often for the present inevitable, society need not itself inflict them. The injudiciousness of parents, a youth's own inexperience, or the absence of external opportunities for the congenial vocation, and their presence for an uncongenial, condemn numbers of men to pass their lives in doing one thing reluctantly and ill, when there are other things which they could have done well and happily. But on women this sentence is imposed by actual law, and by customs equivalent to law. What, in unenlightened societies, colour, race, religion, or in the case of a conquered country, nationality, are to some men, sex is to all women; a peremptory exclusion from almost all honourable occupations, but either such as cannot be fulfilled by others, or such as those others do not think worthy of their acceptance. Sufferings arising from causes of this nature usually meet with so little sympathy, that few persons are aware of the great amount of unhappiness even now produced by the feeling of a wasted life. The case will be even more frequent, as increased cultivation creates a greater and greater disproportion between the ideas and faculties of women, and the scope which society allows to their activity.

When we consider the positive evil caused to the disqualified half of the human race by their disqualification—first in the loss of the most inspiriting and elevating kind of personal enjoyment, and next in the weariness, disappointment, and profound dissatisfaction with life, which are so often the substitute for it; one feels that among all the lessons which men require for carrying on the struggle against the inevitable imperfections of their lot on earth, there is no lesson which they more need, than not to add to the evils which nature inflicts, by their jealous and prejudiced restrictions on one another. Their vain fears only substitute other and worse evils for those which they are idly apprehensive of: while every restraint on the freedom

of conduct of any of their human fellow-creatures (otherwise
than by making them responsible for any evil actually caused
by it), dries up *pro tanto* the principal fountain of human
happiness, and leaves the species less rich, to an inappreci
able degree, in all that makes life valuable to the individual
human being.